The Past Is a Moving Picture

UNIVERSITY PRESS OF FLORIDA

Florida A&M University, Tallahassee
Florida Atlantic University, Boca Raton
Florida Gulf Coast University, Ft. Myers
Florida International University, Miami
Florida State University, Tallahassee
New College of Florida, Sarasota
University of Central Florida, Orlando
University of Florida, Gainesville
University of North Florida, Jacksonville
University of South Florida, Tampa
University of West Florida, Pensacola

UNIVERSITY PRESS
OF FLORIDA
Gainesville
Tallahassee
Tampa
Boca Raton
Pensacola
Orlando
Miami
Jacksonville
Ft. Myers
Sarasota

JANNA JONES

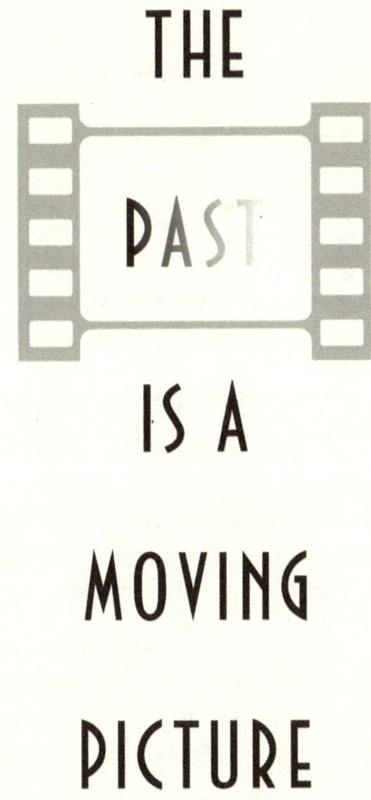

Preserving the Twentieth Century on Film

Printed in the United States of America on acid-free paper

This book may be available in an electronic edition.

First cloth printing, 2012
First paperback printing, 2014

Library of Congress Cataloging-in-Publication Data

Jones, Janna.
The past is a moving picture : preserving the twentieth century on film / Janna Jones.
p. cm.
Includes bibliographical references and index.
Summary: An analysis of how U.S. archivists have not only preserved the history of cinema and of the twentieth century but shaped it as well.
ISBN 978-0-8130-4192-6 (cloth: alk. paper)
ISBN 978-0-8130-6037-8 (pbk.)
1. Motion pictures in historiography. 2. History, Modern—20th century—Historiography. 3. Motion pictures—History—20th century. 4. History in motion pictures. 5. Motion pictures—Archival resources. 6. Motion picture film—Preservation. I. Title.
PN1995.9.H5J64 2012
791.43—dc23
2012009835

University Press of Florida
15 Northwest 15th Street
Gainesville, FL 32611-2079
http://www.upf.com

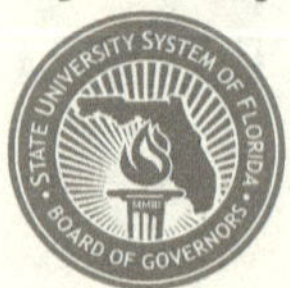

For Mark A. Neumann

Arrange whatever pieces come your way.

Virginia Woolf

CONTENTS

PREFACE

If we can imagine the guardian angel of the moving image archive (perhaps she resembles Iris Barry or maybe Snowden Becker), surely she would be mystified by her present-day duties. As she steadies her gaze upon the accumulation of material she protects, we see her eyes wide in disbelief, her mouth open, slightly aghast. She never imagined it; this angel never thought that she'd have to protect such an overwhelming hoard of images that have amassed at her feet. Like Paul Klee's *Angelus Novus,* she too is caught off guard by the storm of progress. Resisting the winds of progress, Klee's angel would like to be able to close his wings and stay around to commune with the dead. Our guardian angel is not so sure that is a good idea. In her angelic domain, progress is the salvation of the past, not its obliteration. But she has grown weary of tending to the overpopulated spirit world living in the archive. Exhausted, she worries about the sky-high pile of moving images at her feet, our vision of progress in the early twenty-first century.

ACKNOWLEDGMENTS

Many people helped me write this book. I would like to take this moment to thank them. The University of South Florida generously funded my travel to the Library of Congress, the Museum of Modern Art, and the University of California, Los Angeles. The University of South Florida Department of Communication and the School of Communication at Northern Arizona University have also supported this project in many ways.

I had much to learn about the moving image archive as I set about writing this book. I am grateful for the many people who pointed me in all the right directions. I am indebted to Karan Sheldon and David Weiss who welcomed me to Northeast Historic Film, opened many archival doors for me, and patiently answered all my questions during the last five or six years. I am also thankful for the insights and encouragement I have received from Snowden Becker, Liz Coffey, Chris Horak, Jane Johnson Otto, Rick Prelinger, Dwight Swanson, Dan Streible, and Katie Trainor.

I had the good fortune to interview many talented people working in archives all across the country. Their contributions to this book are immense. I would particularly like to thank Arlene Balansky, Mary Lea Bandy, David Francis, Jere Guildin, Steve Leggett, Alan Lewis, Pat Loughney, Greg Lukow, Mike Mashon, Eddie Richmond, Paul Spehr, Jennifer Teely, Ken Weissman, Todd Wiener, Jim Williamson, Peter Williamson, Pam Wintle, and Mark Quigley.

I am deeply grateful for the good humor, encouragement, and support of my friends, Wendy Adams, Karina Aveyard, Mariaelena Bartesaghi, Elizabeth Bell, Kate Bowles, Kris Byrd, Annie Cattan, Marcy Chvasta, Dominique Desjeux, David Eason, Liz Edgecomb, Kristi Frazier, Laura Gray Rosendale, Chris Green, Mary Gould, Erica Hamilton, Paul Helford, Elizabeth Hellstern, Jennifer Jenkins, Robin Jones, Bob Kerstein, Christine Kiesinger, Astrid Klocke, Kurt Lancaster, Michael LeVan, Linda Levitt, Lexa Murphy, David Payne, Stephanie Petrie, Keelyn Riley, Rich Rogers, Steve Rosendale, Ella Schmidt, Tara Schroeder, Julie Schutten, Laura Smith, Mary Tolan, Jon Torn, and Michelle Zacks.

I am humbled and full of gratitude for Mark Jancovich and Albert Moran's support.

I am proud and thankful that Meredith Morris-Babb is the editor of this book and that we have worked together on two books at the University Press of Florida.

A loving thank you to my family: Rich and Kay Severson, Bob and Kay Jones, Jean Neumann, Lynne Severson, Todd and Missy Severson, Brad and Cindy Severson, Beth Severson, Ron Russell, Peter Neumann, Maria Steele, Rich and Erika Neumann, Scott and Claudia Neumann, and Stacy Neumann and Noah Perlut. And a big thank you to my sister, Julee Jones; when we were little girls, she helped to cultivate my interest in old movies by making me watch *Creature Feature* with her on Friday nights.

I thank my husband and trusted reader, Mark Neumann. I am forever grateful for his love and support of my endeavors, and I admire the way he tears down a barn and reclaims a pasture.

INTRODUCTION

The Past Is a Moving Picture details and interprets the twentieth-century project of preserving moving images. This study is an analysis of some of the major assumptions and paradigmatic shifts about history, cinema, and the moving image archive, prior to the current shift toward digitization. This book frames the twentieth century film archive as a project of history making, an endeavor undertaken by modern men and women who not only have attempted to sustain and fix, but also transform meanings about the twentieth century. Film collecting and preservation has played a national and public role in easing various cultural anxieties and desires during the twentieth century. How and why Americans thought (or did not think) about their cinematic heritage reveals important insights into the nation's views of history making, technology, nationalism, the film industry, and the role of cinema in public life during the twentieth century.

Ushering in the second generation of the film archive in the United States, the United States Congress passed legislation establishing the National Film Preservation Board (NFPB) and National Film Registry at the Library of Congress as part of the National Film Preservation Act of 1988. "The National Film Preservation Act," according to David Francis, the retired chief of the Motion Picture, Broadcasting and Recorded Sound Division, "was guided by the belief that the most important films should be kept and preserved in the form that the team created them and to help the contemporary movie industry be more mindful of the original intentions of filmmakers." Since 1989, the Librarian of Congress James Billington has selected twenty-five films for the National Film Registry each year. He chooses the films based on criteria of aesthetic, historical, or cultural importance. The films named to the registry are deemed worthy of preservation and the library is obligated to do all it can to ensure that they will be preserved in their original film formats. The establishment of the NFPB and a new widespread national focus on honoring, maintaining, and recovering the intent of filmmakers moved the Library of Congress's Motion Picture, Broadcasting and Recorded Sound Division into a national spotlight. The library was pushed to the forefront of the film archiving movement in the United States because the library's film collection is widely recognized, Francis told me, as "immense, valuable, and important."

Shortly after the creation of the National Film Registry, the Library of Congress and American Movie Classics, the AMC cable network, developed a nationwide film preservation tour. The tour exhibited National Registry films in theaters around the United States in an effort to educate the public about film preservation and offered them cinematic experiences with preserved films. But the tour was also a public relations campaign. Francis told me that the library wanted it to have better and more complex interactions with the American public, so the tour was developed, in part, to give a public face to the Library of Congress. Regrettably, a lack of resources brought an end to the tour before the registry films were exhibited in all fifty states.

The tour was elaborate, requiring appropriate venues for the exhibition of preserved films, guest speakers, and a spokesperson from the Library of Congress. Many of the film titles were chosen, to some extent, for their canonical stature. Film historians, archivists, and the public generally acknowledge the historical and cultural significance of such films and directors as *The River* (Pare Lorentz, 1937), *Shadow of a Doubt* (Alfred Hitchcock, 1943), *My Darling Clementine* (John Ford, 1946), *The Night of the Hunter* (Charles Laughton, 1955), *Gigi* (Vincente Minnelli, 1958), *Touch of Evil* (Orson Welles, 1958), *2001: A Space Odyssey* (Stanley Kubrick, 1968),

China Town (Roman Polanski, 1974), and *Raging Bull* (Martin Scorsese, 1980). Given the desire to attract the public, the selection is not surprising. The library wanted to educate people about film preservation, and the tour's films were selected to attract a wide and diverse audience.

When the National Film Registry tour came to the Tampa Theatre, I saw *The Great Train Robbery* (Edwin Porter, 1903) and fifty feet of Edison footage depicting troops unloading cargo from a train in Tampa during the Spanish-American War. Together these two films offered the registry tour audience a sample of both historic completeness and fragmentation; the canonical and the obscure linked as film history. Film students and scholars regard *The Great Train Robbery* as a foundational film in the history of narrative cinema, and it is widely recognized as a milestone in film history. Part of the paper print collection at the Library of Congress, *The Great Train Robbery* was deposited for copyright at the library in 1903. The first preservation of the film was done in 1962, resulting in viewing prints (both 16 mm and 35 mm) deposited at the library. The library's film lab did preservation work on the film again in 1987, resulting in a master positive print and several viewing prints. The Museum of Modern Art gave the Library of Congress a theatrical projection print in 1995, and the library's film lab made another viewing copy and master in 2006.[1] The consistency of the library's preservation efforts suggests that both the history and the future of *The Great Train Robbery* are safeguarded. Its history is well documented and widely circulated; its future ensured by custodians who protect, preserve, and duplicate its physical properties.

The Edison footage is more concealed; it is not entirely comprehensible as history. Filmed in May 1898, the thirty-second footage of troops unloading cargo hardly registers as more than a documented event. Like *The Great Train Robbery,* the footage was a Library of Congress copyright deposit (in 1898) and is part of the paper print collection, but much less attention has been paid to it during the last one hundred years. The only preservation work completed on it was a dupe negative and reference print in 1962.[2] David Francis introduced the 1898 Edison film at the Tampa Theatre. The images were difficult to discern, but I could see men loading cargo onto a train, and the footage drew me in. I had seen plenty of still images of Tampa, Florida, at the turn of the twentieth century, but these moving images resurrected the city and the soldiers in a way that photographs could not.

Edison's moving images of a Tampa that existed one hundred years ago were a compelling reminder of how a city's past can disappear from the landscape and from memory. Perhaps it was just the glimpse of the mundane animated before my eyes, but the images also suggested that the past could be summoned by way of the archival moving image, if only in such moments of exhibition. In Edison's filmic minute, I experienced both the loss and a partial salvaging of time. "To look back into the reality of that lost world by means of the cinema," Laura Mulvey writes, "is to have the sensation of looking into a time machine. However clichéd the concept, the presence of that reality, of the past preserved, becomes increasingly magical and uncanny."[3] Witnessing the reanimation of the soldiers, the city, and the era to which the film belonged, I understood that cinema and its preservation have drastically altered our relationship with the past, for it is only we, twenty-first century beings, who experience both the pleasure and the anxiety of watching the century before us come into motion. This moving image time machine has and will continue to have an enormous impact on the way the twentieth century is remembered. But the stakes are high for this sort of history making: the films that are saved, preserved, and made accessible are the ones that will help us to remember particular social, political, and cinematic pasts. The ones that are not will vanish, their film elements quietly disintegrating, their stories disappearing into oblivion.

The National Film Registry films were survivors. The two train films seemed like rare jewels; some of the few precious remains left of the earliest days of cinema. The tour's rhetoric suggested that our film history was in great peril and that much of the moving image evidence of the twentieth century had already disappeared. This scarcity paradigm did, in fact, fuel archival principles during much of the twentieth century. And while scarcity remains foundational to contemporary archival ideology, present-day archives are more likely to be constrained by a proliferation of materials, inadequate funding, and an insufficient number of employees. Efforts to manage today's archives are often thwarted by an overwhelming amount of moving images requiring accession, cataloging, and storage. As a result, there is little archival knowledge about a sizable proportion of materials housed in vaults across the United States. Flagship films with well-defined histories, like *The Great Train Robbery,* are the archival exception rather than the rule. An excess of barely identified moving images lingering in vaults resist archivists and researchers' efforts to make comprehensible both the archive and the United States' cinematic past.

Cinema, of course, appeared on the cultural landscape only a few years prior to the twentieth century. It was not too much later, shortly after movies became commonplace, that people became interested and concerned about saving films. While the film archive is a project that naturally shares some of the same curatorial impulses as other kinds of preservation work that caught hold centuries earlier (buildings, paintings, and documents, for example), it is an undertaking unique to the twentieth century. Cinema itself is a modern idea; it is a mechanically produced (and reproduced) form of art and entertainment that was widely distributed and consumed by the masses throughout the twentieth century. Cinema's production of technological stimulation, continuous movement and re-presentation of reality, as Leo Charney and Vanessa Schwartz explain, "are a crucible of elements already evident in other aspects of modern culture, cinema accidentally outpaced these other forms, ending up as far more than just another novel gadget."[4] Miriam Bratu Hansen argues that cinema "was above all (at least until the rise of television) the single most expansive discursive horizon in which the effects of modernity were reflected, rejected or denied, transmuted or negotiated."[5]

Many theorists and critics, who have deliberated on cinema through the lens of modernity, consider cinema's necessary interrelationship with capitalism's mass production, distribution, reception, as well as its potential for unraveling capitalism itself. The Frankfurt School's Theodor Adorno and Max Horkheimer found cinema to be a commodity that tried to mimic art, but was simply part of the culture industry that created trivial and comfortable cultural products. Their contemporaries Siegfried Kracauer and Walter Benjamin considered cinema's form, content, and effects of spectatorship, believing that it could help us understand the modern age—offering us a way, at least, to discover modernity's trap doors. The young Kracauer explained that cinema characterized modernity because it both attracted and represented the masses, but he also believed that it "constitutes the most advanced cultural institution in which the masses, as a relatively heterogeneous, undefined, and unknown form of collectivity, can represent themselves as a *public* (author's emphasis)."[6] Benjamin thought film was not only an outcome of mechanical reproduction, but that it was inherent in its form. He argued that cinema, a product of modernity's making, could represent the masses as a collective and had the potential to revolutionize the proletariat, thus destroying capitalism with its own form of production.

Both Kracauer and Benjamin were fascinated with film's structure and content, believing that cinema's transformation of time and space had much to reveal about the subjective experience of modernity. Theorists of modernity have focused upon chance, the contingent, and the indeterminate, an experience of time that seems to defy standardization and rationalization of the temporal. Industrial life, from the efficiency of the laborer's body in the factory to the railroad's re-organization of time for efficient scheduling to the popularization of the pocket watch, created a logical, public ordering of time. The same modern impulses that created temporal rationalization also created a nearly incomprehensible transformation in the way people experienced time in their private lives. The spectacle-filled city with its density and its anonymous nature, rapid industrialization, and the dissemination of modern transportation and technologies produced the experience of shock, the momentary, the contingent, and the ephemeral for the modern subject.

Benjamin, as well as many scholars who followed him, thought cinema, like the railroad, the streetcar, industrial organization and the confusion, congestion, and anonymity of urban life, reflected, challenged, and also helped to transform modern life, eliminating traditional barriers of space and time and effecting overstimulation, distraction, and shock. In his often quoted observation about cinema's impact on modern experience Benjamin writes, "Then came the film and burst this prison-world asunder by the dynamite of the tenth of a second, so that now, in the midst of its far-flung ruins and debris, we calmly and adventurously go traveling."[7] Kracauer imagined that film spectators in the cinema house experienced film in much the same way as they did modern life, with contingency and indeterminacy, a meandering not unlike that of Benjamin's flaneur. "Does the spectator ever succeed in exhausting the objects he contemplates?" Kracauer asks. "There is no end to his meanderings. Sometimes, though, it may seem to him that, after having probed a thousand possibilities, he is listening, with all of his senses strained, to a confused murmur."[8]

Cinema as an experiential analog to the way time and space had become organized in urban life created a nearly seamless continuity between the city streets and what transpired on film and in the movie theater. Motion pictures, in the early twentieth century, captured the transformation of modern experience. Films revealed, in shadows and light, a reorganization of the subject as a spectator, as a person for whom the idea of time had become pliable and comprehensible in so many arrangements and discontinuities. Cinema was a formidable subject for theorists such as Kracauer and Benjamin as it captured the "here and now" (which immediately becomes the "there and then"), and it paralleled the transformation of the modern spectator who, more often than not, was imagined as part of the mass culture. Cinema, then, for some cultural theorists in the first half of the twentieth century was met with ambivalence. It had revolutionary potential to liberate the masses, but it was also viewed as a way to contain them. In other words, the populist character of motion pictures was both a problem and a possibility. To be clear, filmgoers did not confront cinema with this sort of ambiguity and intellectual curiosity. For most cinemagoers, during this same period, film was a spectacular event, both for what they saw on the screen, as well as the social interactions available in and around the movie theater.

When we consider the ways that some leading intellectuals were confronting film during the first half of the twentieth century, we can better appreciate the visionary perspectives of early twentieth-century proponents of film preservation who would ultimately rescue some of the country's earliest cinema from demise. While early preservationists were intent on preserving America's newest form of art, news, and entertainment, with all of its scenes, stories, and stars, they were also by default preserving the experience of the early twentieth-century subject. At the same time, early film collecting (as well as all film preservation throughout the twentieth century) was an attempt to culturally elevate the moving image, for any object worth preserving, is an object of some cultural import.

The twentieth-century quest to archive film is a curious history-making endeavor that embraces the systemization and rationalization of traditional archival projects. However, efforts to ensure that the twentieth-century moving image did not disappear depended and still depends upon a source that is itself contingent, momentary. The nature of film's materiality is fragile, ephemeral, and short-lived. While other objects that are routinely preserved such as buildings, books, paintings, sculptures, documents, and costumes are also subject to deterioration and decay, they are not as fragile as celluloid. They have longevity. Nitrate film, the film stock of the first half of the twentieth century, essentially begins to decompose the moment it is manufactured. In addition, without proper care, it has the potential to spontaneously combust. Nitrate's successor, safety film that appeared during the second half of the twentieth century, also has the tendency to disintegrate without proper care, as a result of a catalytic reaction in its base, which causes disintegration. The film archive, then, from its beginning was like containing and preserving the twentieth century with books written in disappearing ink.

The film archive that has sought to preserve the filmic world of the twentieth century is a project that is as nearly complicated as modernity itself. While critics and theorists have necessarily looked to cinema as a way to make sense of temporal and spatial shifting taking place in modernity, my focus on how and why archivists and film preservationists have attempted to save cinema sheds new light on how modern people imagined and then created a way to confront, reveal, confine, and hold on to the recent past. In other words, this is a study of how modern people apprehended the past and conceptualized and enacted history making, by way of the film archive. It details archivists' and preservationists' perceptions and methodologies for securing artifacts that they deemed culturally and cinematically significant so to understand how they negotiated the present and imagined the future, while laying claim to the past. As the historian William Cummings has argued, there is a valuable contribution to be made by focusing on how the past is understood. "Surely it is here in this activity, in questions of what the past means and what people in the present do with the past, that the epistemological status and knowledge of the past converge."[9]

While archivists and preservationists are not historians in the traditional sense, neither are they the historian's handmaidens. Through their systematic gathering and preserving of filmic objects they have constructed an exemplification, a representation, and a chronicle of the twentieth century that in and of itself is an act of interpretive history making. Twentieth-century archivists created a particular kind of historical text that is as unique to the twentieth century as film itself. The archive is generally considered to be the historian's source for making meaning. The historian selects what is believed to be most significant from the archive and imposes meaning upon it by creating a narrative, the form of representation that most historians utilize. Archivists and preservationists are usually considered the guardians of the past and not the interpreters of it; yet, as this work demonstrates, during the last century they systematically interpreted the past by collecting and organizing a distinctive artifact, using a unique historical method that ultimately created a peculiar narrative specific to the history of the twentieth century.

The archive, as I have already stated, is generally considered a repository for accessing materials that help to shape history, but the film archive is not only a storehouse, it is also a colossal historical text of words and images. The image-based archive intermingles with the textual information contained within it: cataloging information, contextual information, websites, databases, and, of course, traditionally written histories written by film scholars and archivists. The written texts and cinematic images of the archive come together to form a filmic discourse unique to the twentieth century. It is a history-making project unlike any other and its potential for discovery, interpretation, re-presentation, and accessing the timbre of the past is one that is barely understood at the beginning of the twenty-first century.

Archives are often considered to be rational, scientific, and disciplined spaces; their formation and evolution shaped by a cultural logic paralleled by a culture's dominant historical narratives. The moving image archive, in many ways, conforms to this popular understanding. However, almost from the beginning, the practices and principles driving moving image archives have been intuitive and rational, chaotic and disciplined. A dialectic of creation and destruction, control and chaos has shaped the twentieth-century moving image archive, resulting in an environment of logic and ingenuity, as well as order and disruption. During the twentieth century, a relatively small group of people had hopes and fears about film that fostered great archival intent. Decaying and disappearing films haunted some. Others pushed to save and protect films because they believed they had the power to instruct and persuade. Most thought that old films were a remedy to cultural amnesia. Many of the people that influenced the shape of the moving image archive during the twentieth century were in positions of power at cultural institutions such as the Library of Congress, the Museum of Modern Art, and the National Archives. Yet, their archival desire, training, education, power, and knowledge were not always enough.

Despite archivists' best efforts to tame and rationalize the moving image archive, it has not always cooperated. This is not to say that the archival intent of the twentieth century was in vain. Rather, the dialectic forces that have shaped the moving-image archive have created an environment where a coherent and unified story of cinema's past does not easily take root. The archive may strive toward static and finite interpretations of the past, but it also cultivates ongoing, contingent, and inconclusive attitudes toward moving image history making.

As film archivists gradually (at first) and then rapidly (in the last decades of the century) built collections, they constructed a dense, chaotic, and eclectic representation of the United States. The filmic content and aesthetics contained within the cinematic archive embody the visual experience of the twentieth century. A massive compilation of images, the film archive is also a complex montage network—not the montage within the films—though that is relevant, too, but rather the montage between films. The archive contains high culture, low culture, and every cultural representation in between: actualities, art films, government films, newsreels, amateur movies, Hollywood films, pornography, and experimental films comingle, prohibiting us from constructing any sort of unified, cohesive view of the twentieth century by way of the entirety of its contents.

As the twentieth century progressed and certainly by the century's end, the film archive in the United States became a massive text that embodies, even exceeds, Benjamin's historiographic intentions. Walter Benjamin rejected historicism for its privileging of progress and the future, and its narrative construction that represents the past, present, and future in a natural, determined, and smoothed-out trajectory. Benjamin's theorization of culture and modernity included a preoccupation with historiography and the ways in which historicism shaped and repressed modern consciousness. Born to a bourgeois Jewish family in Berlin in 1892 and living in the crossfire of Germany's ideological madness, Benjamin experienced firsthand the destructive effects of historicism.

Disallowing historical thinking that privileged the victors of the past and killed off, once more, those who were trampled and destroyed by those in power, Benjamin hoped to redeem the fragments of the past rather than using them for the purpose of propelling present ideologies into the victories of the future. Because Benjamin rejected historicism in favor of a historical practice that redeemed the past, he conceived of new methodologies for writing history that aimed to awaken his readers from their deep sleep. Benjamin envisioned the writing of history as a shock-inducing form, similar in some ways to the shocks people were experiencing in modern life. Benjamin utilized this principle of interruption, literary montage, as a historical method particularly in *The Arcades Project,* the book he was working on at the time of his death.

The Arcades Project, Benjamin's counterforce to historicism, is a cultural history that focuses on nineteenth-century Paris and its arcades (showplaces of Parisian consumerism, spectacle, distraction, and alluring commodities that prefigured twentieth-century malls), street plans of Paris, urban gardens, interiors of bourgeois homes, fashion, iron-and-glass architecture, photography, and prostitution. He also focuses on Parisian types: the flaneur, the gambler, and the collector. Benjamin takes into account these various, even scattered subjects to make sense of the cultural, social, and political daily life of nineteenth-century capitalist modernity. Benjamin's narrative form is a series of citations, cataloging, extracts, notes, and commentaries, which confounds the traditional historical narrative. It seems that Benjamin wishes for the citations, the traces of nineteenth-century Paris, to speak for themselves. However, he also produces theoretical commentary about the historical remains of which he cites, intertwining that which seems to need no commentary with his theorization of them.

Benjamin's montage-like narrative in *The Arcades Project* interrogates conventional historiography by privileging what remains of the past, rather than synthesizing them into a tidy narrative that closes off history for the ideological demands of the present. He "shows" as much as he "tells" upending and destabilizing the traditional historical sequence so that historical time cannot be fixed and finalized. Benjamin did select and prioritize his citations disallowing all that remains of the past to speak entirely for itself. "But the sheer bulk of citations," Philip Rosen explains, "is itself a formal blockage to any smooth historiographic sublimation. The form of the text foregrounds the 'documents,' refusing to subsume them under a sublimating umbrella temporality."[10] *The Arcades Project* was likely not completed at the time that Walter Benjamin committed suicide in 1940. We do not know what he had planned for its completion, but its state of incompletion mirrors his view of historical understanding. Its unfinishedness, then, seems to be exactly the point. Its indeterminacy resists historicism and its march of progress that Benjamin saw as culminating in war, death, and destruction.

Benjamin's historical understanding centered upon montage because he believed modernity was shaped by the visual, the spectacle and its fragmentary nature. "For Benjamin," Schwartz explains, "the fragment established itself as the trope of the modern. Histories would need to be written not only *for* their times but to embody the *forms* of their times if awakening (the goal of history) was to be achieved."[11] Benjamin believed that we could never step into the past on its terms. In *The Arcades Project* and elsewhere he viewed the past as an image that flashes up and can be seized by the present in what he calls the "dialectical image." Confronting the past as an image, Benjamin writes, "For while the relation of the present to the past is a purely temporal, continuous one, the relation of what-has-been to the now is dialectical; is not progression but image, suddenly emergent."[12]

Objects from the past are seized up out of the past and understood in the present, without a sense of continuity between the past and present, so to avoid the historical continuum of which Benjamin was so opposed. As Susan Buck-Morss explains: "Benjamin was counting on the shock of this recognition to jolt the dreaming collective into a political 'awakening.' The presentation of the historical object within a charged field of past and present, which produces political electricity in a 'lightning flash' of truth, is the 'dialectical image.'"[13] Benjamin likened his methodology to a stereoscope, a visual instrument that produces a three-dimensional image by way of juxtaposing two images. In *The Arcades Project,* Benjamin provided one image of the stereoscope, the facts of nineteenth-century Paris; the reader was to provide the other from the images of his or her lived experience. These two images together create the stereoscopic image or the clash between an object's prior life and its reception in the present. This stereoscopic "now-time," is the shock of modernity's cultural consciousness, which seems to be the only way that Benjamin believed we could be awakened, the only way that we could understand the truth.

Benjamin, of course, was not alone in his focus on form and re-formulation. Modern writers, dancers, filmmakers, musicians, and artists during the same era were experimenting with radical new forms attempting to discover art forms that mirrored the crisis of perception, experience, and modernity. Benjamin, Howard Eiland argues, was not only attempting to make himself at home in the world's ontological scatter, but also trying to make that ontological scatter accessible in *The Arcades Project.* Eiland further explains:

> To be sure, this project as a whole, with its persistent documentary intention and its improvisatory arrangement of materials (an arrangement dictated mainly, it appears, by the course of Benjamin's studies) would seem to combine the most concrete sort of content with the most indeterminate sort of form. But perhaps it can be said that the montage of fragments (excerpts and reflections) which Benjamin has assembled in this text—assuming that it *is* a text, at least de facto, and not just a notebook—does work soberly to mirror the scatteredness of things, especially things perceived in an urban environment, and, as it were, en passant.[14]

Cinema is obviously a significant model for Benjamin's dialectical image and his conceptualization of literary montage for the writing of *The Arcades Project*. Montage, an aesthetic of modernity, offers Benjamin a way of representing intermediary spatial and temporal positions that enable readers to at least momentarily position themselves in such a way that they are able to permeate the past and the present simultaneously. Schwartz argues Benjamin's notions of history as guided by cinema offer us a mode and medium through which to awaken from the collective sleep that Benjamin delineates. She writes, "If film is both like history in that it represents an absence and unlike history in that it seems to erase the pastness of the past, it may very well embody the 'Now of recognizability' that Benjamin described as what emerges from his notion of 'dialectics at a standstill.' In this way, film becomes a key mode of historical awakening."[15]

The film archive, particularly during its second wave and at the beginning of the twenty-first century, is in a constant state of unfinishedness. Its relentless destabilization, incomplete films, always decaying matter, filmic materials stacked to roof tops, and partial (at best) documentation is a constant source of frustration for archivists around the country, and it mightily challenges their patience and faith; yet, the undetermined state of the archive, its contingent nature, and its resistance to discipline challenges historicism. This extraordinary filmic discourse is impossible to solidify; its strewn thick images and texts resist containment, mirroring the scattered, decontextualized consciousness of modernity while simultaneously defying fixed and singular meanings of history. Make no mistake about it, those who work in the film archive do not celebrate the liberating potential of the filmic discourse that they attempt to systematically create and protect. The current film archive in the United States, in fact, fails to measure up to anything close to an archival ideal. But it comes much closer to perfecting the Benjaminian ideal. The current film archive, then, is the perfect unmanageable and incomplete history-making project of the twentieth century.

To be sure, almost all contemporary scholars focus on the problems rather than the liberating possibilities of the archive. Jacques Derrida's *Archive Fever: A Freudian Impression* has influenced many contemporary researchers' understanding of the archive as both a metaphor and literal space of power. "There is no political power without control of the archive, if not memory," Derrida proclaims. "Effective democratization can always be measured by this essential criterion: the participation in and access to the archive, its constitution, and its interpretation."[16] Derrida's archival theory is partially based in Freudian analysis, particularly the counteractive forces of the death drive and the conservation drive, or the pleasure principal. Freud's death drive: the urge toward destruction incites "the annihilation of memory." The archive, according to Derrida, is not spontaneous or alive memory. He explains, "On the contrary: the archive takes place at the place of originary and structural breakdown of the said memory."[17] Marlene Manoff contends that the stakes of this struggle, the negotiation between the death drive and the pleasure principal, can be quite high. "In the aftermath of the U.S. led 'Operation Iraqi Freedom,' Iraq's National Museum, National Library, National Archives and other repositories have been looted and burned," Manoff writes. "A chorus of voices has declared this a cultural disaster of immense proportion."[18] But Derrida's ideas can also help to uncover the significance of other, much smaller struggles over the meaning and definition of the collection or the archive. "Derrida's work has contributed to scholarly recognition of the contingent nature of the archive," asserts Manoff, "the way it is shaped by social, political, and technological forces."[19]

Scholars throughout the twentieth century have wrestled with their definitions and critiques of the modern archive. For the first half of the twentieth century, scholars generally viewed the traditional archive as a neutral repository for artifacts that enabled historians to interpret history. Following the work of the renowned French historian Marc Bloch (1886–1944), scholars understood that the archive's authority was derived primarily from scholarly interpretations of archival materials, rather than any authority contained within the archive itself.[20] But when Michel Foucault began publishing his work on the clinic and the archeological order of things, the archive's neutrality and its innocence was upturned.[21] Foucault and the scholars that followed him argued that the archive, far from being a neutral site, gained authority by way of policing, surveillance, empire building, and governmentality. Since Foucault, scholars have increasingly viewed the archive itself as an object of study, interpreting it as an authoritative site whereby materials are collected, contained, and disciplined in order to create histories of those in power. Nicholas Dirks, for example, contends that the archive "produces, adjudicates, organizes, and maintains discourses that become available as the 'primary' texts of history."[22] The archive, according to Dirks and others following Foucault, authorizes its contents by fixing meaning with exactitude and irrevocability.[23] The archive disciplines its materials in such a way that any knowledge derived from the archive is necessarily sanctioned.

Some postcolonial scholars view the archive as a site that asserts discipline through its omissions, categories, and rules but is somewhat ineffectual in maintaining its prescribed meanings, particularly once materials fall into the hands of nonauthorities and the intended and unintended archival users. Some scholars working to uncover the disciplinary procedures and operations of the archive (particularly the British archive of the nineteenth century) contend that the archive's attempts to privilege the history of those in power is only partially successful.[24] "No doubt, then, the archive has often been set up precisely to exclude those regarded as marginal or threatening to the business of rule," argues Phillipa Levine. "But there is a huge gulf between desiring to silence and successfully silencing, and we can surely no longer argue that the archive, however constructed, continues to exert such power in monochromatic ways."[25]

But the act of archiving is a process of constructing reality from a particular social position and point of view. Richard Brown and Beth Davis-Brown explain that the "technical-rational work" of the archivist may not be overtly political, but it does shape national public memory. The unrecognized, undetected functions of the archive must be uncovered, they claim, so that we may better understand the ideological nature of past decisions and practices.[26] The history of the archive is an amalgam of conservation and loss that is not only shaped by determination and ideological power.

Paul Voss and Marta Werner suggest that some losses and omissions are merely accidental. Other absences come about as a result of the inability to tame the archive. "Even if the historical winds never destabilized the archives, their ultimate stability would not be guaranteed: the archive's dream of perfect order is disturbed by the nightmare of its random, heterogeneous, and often unruly contents," Voss and Werner write. "The dream of those secret or disconcerting elements ('errors,' 'garbage') located at its outermost edges or in its deepest recesses defie codification and unsettle memory and context."[27] While Voss and Werner hope to widen our understanding of who and what shapes the archive, like Derrida and others, they suggest that we must also take into account the contingencies that shape the archive and cultural memory.

The poetics of archival exclusion may include historical accidents, but David Greetham also argues that we cannot ignore the predictability of archival construction, which he likens to the act of book editing. Both the acts of archiving and editing, he argues, are likely to be culturally commendable, insidious, repressive, and restrictive.[28] Cultural conservators' practices and values are invariably rooted in exclusion and inequity, he contends, for rather than gathering together everything, they focus on archiving what they understand to be the *best* of everything. Cultural collecting is both "self-referential" and "self-laudatory" he claims. Like the space probe miniarchive that was shot off into the solar system, the archive is "a sort of Arnoldian best that was ever thought and known in the world."[29] Furthermore, Greetham contends that it is folly to predict what will and will not be important in the future. "The cultural poetics is heavily dependent not only on historical accidents of transmission but on various types of agency that receive cultural prerogatives at particular times," Greetham writes. "And while the prerogatives bestowed by culture may often have been taken seriously by the standards of the time, attempts either to predict the archival needs of the future or to find universalist systems of classification are inherently doomed by the force of local prejudice."[30]

Like every other imaginable arena of contested space, scholars have attempted to complicate our understanding of the ideological nature of the archive. It is not surprising at all that the archives are sites of struggle. Rather than offer a politically unified vision, the archive can or may be a site of struggle and contestation of power. Michael Lynch recommends that scholars interested in the meaning of the archive study the "work of assembling, disrupting, and reconfiguring particular archival collections." He claims that such studies should be seen as "historical phenomena in their own right." "Such an orientation does not negate the scholarly use of archival information; instead, it shifts attention to archives *in formation* and the localized gathering of histories."[31] Rather than theorize the archive from above, Lynch suggests scholars climb into the archival trenches so to better understand the archive as a site with its own specific histories of alliance, resistance, and contingency. If we understand the archive as a site with its own histories, we can better know the histories of which the archive is a custodian.

Because my work focuses on how people assemble, consider, employ, and attempt to contain the past in the present, I am aware of my own archiving here. This is a particular set of narratives to tell the story of the twentieth-century moving image archive. It is not my intention, nor do I think it is possible, to tell a definitive and comprehensive story of the moving image archive. Instead I focus on the policy studies, public hearings, legislation, and archival principles at prominent archival institutions that have had the cultural authority to both theorize and realize the moving image archive in the United States. These national and regional efforts as well as the authoritative archival discourse they have generated tell a compelling account of the United States' evolving relationship with both cinema and the archive during the twentieth century.

The first part of *The Past Is a Moving Picture* (Archives in Formation) interprets significant public discourse surrounding the first wave of the film archive. It focuses on how and why archivists, the federal government, film industry leaders, and scholars in the United States advocated for the collecting of cinema. Today, the archiving community considers this period of amassing materials and formulating collection policies to be the first generation of the film archive (1930s to late 1980s). The first generation of film archivists were primarily film collectors whose concerns focused primarily on what kind of films should be collected, for whom they should be collected, and what kinds of knowledge could be gleaned from the collections. If the first wave created knowledge by way of public discourse and acquisition, the second wave (late 1980s to present) of film archivists are constructing the history of the twentieth century by way of their attention to, maintenance, preservation, and restoration of archival film materials. Archivists who have been trained to properly manage and preserve film materials have replaced the archive's first wave collectors who are sometimes remembered as secretive protectors of their collections rather than conscientious custodians of their materials.

While the public exhibition of cinema had existed for less than a half of a century, during the 1920s through the 1940s, leaders in the film industry and some of the country's most powerful cultural institutions recognized cinema's potential as a nationalistic tool for boosting the United States' cultural and political identity. In chapter 1 ("What to Show the World") I explain that the origins of the film archive were guided by historicism's impulses. During this time, film archiving was primarily defined by the institutional attempts of the Library of Congress, the National Archives, and the Museum of Modern Art to build national film collections for the purpose of enhancing the reputation of the United States to both its own citizens and to the rest of the world. The various attempts at creating national film collections during the first wave of the archive were not entirely successful, but they did create both the public awareness and a new rhetoric to help save the country's early cinema. While the nationalistic undercurrent of the archive's first generation eventually dissipated, the first wave's collecting and rhetorical contributions helped to build the foundation for the contemporary United States film archive.

The relationship between consumer capitalism, technological innovation, and film access is a troubling one for the archive at the beginning of the twenty-first century, but the roots of this conundrum began decades before the onset of the Internet revolution. In chapter 2 ("Accessibility, Authenticity, and Anxiety") I focus on the creation of the American Film Institute (AFI) in the 1960s and the colorization controversy of the 1980s and how these events opened the door to both the potential and the problems of archival accessibility. Guided by the New Frontier philosophy and the film industry's capital, the AFI sought inexpensive film-viewing technologies so that students and filmmakers would have easy access to films. The AFI cracked open the ideological gates for archival accessibility, ushering in a new archival principle that became a reality a decade or so after the AFI became an institution. However, as the colorization controversy revealed, the innovative technologies that brought about the ability to replicate and exhibit films inexpensively also created the capacity for people outside of the archival setting to alter the content and meanings of canonical films. This archival threat revealed the ways that classic

Hollywood films had become a part of the nation's popular memory and also had the potential to generate profit for those who owned the rights to them. Colorization technology also revealed a significant and troubling fact about the cinematic artifact: powerful people and new technologies could dramatically alter films sitting safely in the archive. The film archive, as we can see on YouTube each day, hardly guarantees a fixed and stable cinematic memoryscape.

While the second wave of the film archive began in the late 1980s, it was in full throttle in 1993 when the National Film Preservation Board held two public hearings about the current state of American film preservation. In chapter 3 ("Film Preservation 1993: Orphans and the Culture Wars") I interpret the archival discourse at the congressional hearings as an indirect outcome of the culture wars and the Christian Right's successful attack on the National Endowment for the Arts, the primary funder of film preservation in the United States. Federal funding for preservation had been drastically reduced at the same time that the film archive was increasingly understood as the memoryscape of the twentieth century. Part of the purpose of the hearings (and the report that followed) was an attempt to redirect the federal government's preservation priorities from Hollywood to orphan films and to shift some of the financial burdens of preservation onto film studios.

Paramount to the hearings' discourse was that all American citizens might shape their historical consciousness by accessing a wide array of cinematic genres, and for the first time in archival history orphan films were discursively placed front and center. The successful paradigmatic shift from a Hollywood-centered preservation plan to an orphan-centered one served to dramatically expand the type and scope of cinematic histories preserved within film archives, ultimately foiling the intentions of the Conservative Right and liberating the effects of historicism from the culture of the film archive in the United States. But the shift hardly lessened the difficulties of the moving image archive. While a lack of cinematic artifacts and public interest had once plagued the archive, at the end of the twentieth century, archivists confronted a new obstacle: artifactual surplus and the increased expectation that the public should have easy access to collections supported with tax dollars.

The last section of *The Past Is a Moving Picture* (Archival Techne) focuses on the labor of the second wave of archivists who have been professionally trained to care for their collections, while also paying close attention to collecting policies and acquiring new film materials. Archivists in the second wave focus much of their attention on film materials already collected (rather than determining what to collect and how to acquire it); thus, it is necessary to turn our attention to archival techne, the science and art of archiving. I interviewed archivists about their work in the archives where they work so to best understand second-wave practices and the ideologies that help to form those practices. While the first part of this study focuses primarily on textual analyses of public discourse, the second part (Archival Techne) is a textual and an ethnographic analysis of recent archival practices so to understand the systems, customs, and the procedures of archiving and the ideology embedded within them.[32] Karen Gracy, an ethnographer who analyzes current film preservation's competing definitions of values, explains that archival ethnography "is a form of naturalistic inquiry which positions the researcher within an archival environment to gain the cultural perspective of those responsible for the creation, collection, care and use of records."[33]

Where archivists and researchers once felt confounded by a lack of artifactual evidence, today, fueled in part by contemporary culture's compulsion to collect, many archives are overflowing with moving images and related artifacts. Chapter 4 ("The Archive at the End of the Century: Discipline, Excess, and Access") reveals the ways in which attempts to manage the archive are routinely thwarted by the overwhelming amount of cinematic materials requiring accession, cataloging, and storage, as well as insufficient funding and archival labor. As a result, ideological formations cannot take hold, making it impossible for the archivists to construct an entirely linear, singular path toward history; instead, the archive tends toward an indeterminate state that cultivates a way of looking at history that is neither fixed nor complete.

While archives can only do restoration work on a small fraction of their holdings, it is work that is central to archive's identity. Restored films can bring acclaim to an archive as well as to the restorationist who does the work. My examination of three restored films and the archivists who restored them in chapter 5 ("Film Restoration: A New Way of Seeing Film History") uncovers the various ways that preservationists wrestle with issues of authenticity and how restorationists literally and metaphorically piece history together. While it is not unusual for archivists to be dissatisfied with their final restorations, I argue that it is precisely the disruptions, illegible moments, and gaps that change and enhance the way we understand a film's history. These restorations suggest that film history is an ongoing and open-ended process whereby future interpretations and alternative meanings of history remain possible.

Although this book focuses on archival eras preceding digitization, I consider the current archival transition from analog to digital. The transition is nascent, but I conclude by taking stock of the challenges and possibilities that archives currently face in a digital era. Digitization creates both an information explosion and an increased threat of information extinction. Digitized archives have the potential to bring a nearly incomprehensible amount of moving images to diverse and vast audiences, but it is expensive, labor intensive, and technologically challenging. Many archives currently face nearly overwhelming obstacles managing their analog collections; the digital transition will more than double the amount of material archivists must manage, while substantially increasing their costs.

The transition, unfortunately, also comes at a time when the federal government is preoccupied with a historic financial crisis. During such times, cultural institutions suffer as the government's priorities are focused on economic stability not heritage. Duplication is integral to the moving image archive's cultural logic. The digital archive, like its analog predecessor, collects and preserves impermanent and ephemeral materials to stave off our impermanence. Collection, inspection, cataloging, storage, preservation, restoration, exhibition, and duplication—these are ways the archive shapes history. These are the ways it is part of the history it shapes. Over and over the archive replicates itself to reassure us that the past will not disappear.

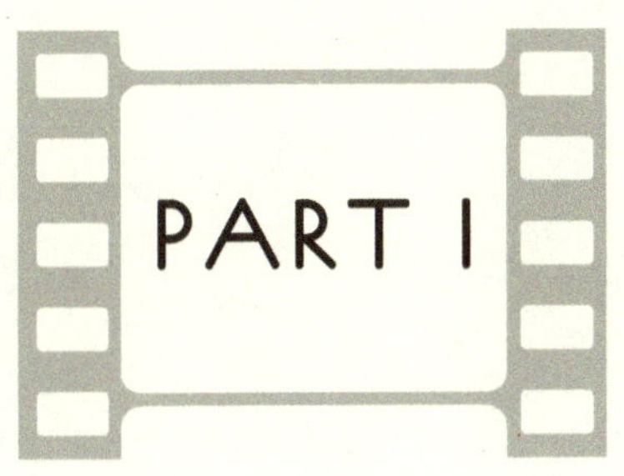

ARCHIVES IN FORMATION

1

WHAT TO SHOW THE WORLD

In the first decade of the twenty-first century, moving image archivists and preservationists are in general agreement about the purpose and cultural significance of their work. The National Film Preservation Foundation (NFPF), the nonprofit created by the United States Congress to help protect the country's cinematic heritage, concisely articulates this agreed upon philosophy. The NFPF notes that Americans have been documenting their worlds with the motion picture camera since 1893. "They captured, with the immediacy unique to the moving image, how generations of Americans have lived, worked, and dreamed," the foundation's website explains. "By preserving these films we save a century of history."[1] For most archivists it seems to go without saying that films are critically important artifacts of the twentieth century.

But archivists rarely focus their public conversations on what seems to be the obvious importance of the moving image historical record; instead they frequently stress that much of the filmic past has vanished and what remains of the cinematic record has the very real potential of disappearing. While no one knows how many films have disappeared entirely, the archival community generally agrees that approximately 10 percent of the films made between 1910 and 1920 still exist; 20 percent of the films made in the 1920s have survived, and only 50 percent of the feature films produced before 1950 remain at least partially intact. There is no way for the archivists to know how many documentaries, shorts, and independent films have entirely disappeared from the cinematic record because their filmmakers rarely left behind documentation and trade magazines infrequently published material about them. The reasons for these numbers are varied, but the fragility and flammability of nitrate film stock and the early studios' general disregard for films after their theatrical run are often noted as primary culprits. During the first years of the twentieth century, films were generally regarded as lowbrow entertainment with little cultural significance. Because they were not valued as an art form or an important part of the cultural landscape, studios, exhibitors, and audiences rarely considered older films worthy of reissuing or preserving.

Recounting her first trip to Hollywood to secure films for the Museum of Modern Art's Film Library, Iris Barry wrote "we soon realized that, perhaps understandably, no one cared a button about 'old' films, not even his own last-but-one, but was solely concerned with his new film now in prospect."[2] Production companies did not want to pay to store the films they released, so negatives and prints were routinely destroyed. Because nitrate film stock was regarded as having more value than the images recorded on them, nitrate film was sold for the silver in its film base. The American Mutoscope and Biograph Company was an important exception. Reissuing short films, primarily D. W. Griffith's films made between the years of 1908–13, the company added new titles to one-reel productions. Film historian Anthony Slide explains they reissued the films not only to double the length of their newer reels, but also because they discovered that audiences enjoyed watching the films of screen stars such as Mary Pickford and Lillian Gish when they were still anonymous actors. "It is perhaps exactly because these American Biograph productions had reissue value that they were cared for and survived," Slide argues, "almost in their entirety, with the majority preserved today at the Museum of Modern Art."[3]

While estimations of nitrate films that have disappeared are frequently cited to support the importance of the archival mission, many films made after the 1950s are missing and are at risk. Eastman Kodak replaced nitrate stock with acetate-based safety film in 1949 in an effort to prevent dangerous nitrate fires and explosions, but safety film, like nitrate, also deteriorates without proper and expensive storage. A disappearing record that archivists believe is as integral to history making as the printed word compels them to collect, protect, preserve, restore, and provide access to the nation's cinematic remains. The coddling of cinematic ruins may seem obvious to the reader, but present-day archivists and preservationists could just as well explain that their mission is to manage the great volume of moving images in their care. Rather than focusing on the absence of cinematic artifacts, they could legitimately state that their mission is to manage an overwhelming amount of material that falls into their hands.

We need only glance at some of the features of the new Library of Congress Packard Campus for Audio-Visual Conservation to see that the present-day archive is hardly void of filmic artifacts. The Packard Campus, located in Culpepper, Virginia, has 90 miles of shelving for collections, 35 climate-controlled vaults, and 124 nitrate vaults. It is the first archive to preserve digital content at the petabyte level (quadrillion bytes). The George Eastman House in Rochester, New York, among the largest moving image archives in the United States has more than 25,000 film titles in its collections. The Museum of Modern Art's Celeste Bartos Film Preservation Center houses its 14,000 titles in vaults of approximately 35,000 square feet in Hamlin, Pennsylvania. The National Archives multimedia collections include almost 300,000 reels of motion picture film and more than 200,000 sound and video recordings. The UCLA Film and Television Archive has more than 220,000 motion picture and television titles and 27 million feet of newsreel footage. While these are some of the most notable (for their size and influence) archives in the country, there are hundreds of other corporate, university, state, and regional archives currently housing millions and millions of feet of film in their vaults. Present-day archivists were quite willing to speak to me about the difficulties of trying to maintain the massive amounts of material in their care, but they rarely mention it when they publicly argue for the importance of preserving cinematic artifacts.

Examining some of the earliest attempts to collect and archive films in the United States prior to the 1950s enables us to interpret the ways that moving images were valued in the initial era of film preservation. Early efforts help make sense of the ways that individuals and cultural institutions made claims about the evidentiary nature of moving images, allowing for a deeper understanding of the evolution of film's value as a cultural object. During a period when the technology and the motion picture industry were still relatively new, some early film collection advocates likened moving images to time travel; future generations would be able to view details of people, daily life, landscapes, and momentous events. Others believed early motion pictures provided the evidence for understanding the cinematic Genesis story. And some believed in the rhetorical power of motion pictures in the present, imagining that they might shape the way other nations viewed the United States. Regardless of which direction early advocates looked, they all saw moving images as evidence that could transcend temporality. Film images, in other words, could attest to the realities of the past even when the spatial fields, objects, and people they depicted had long disappeared.

The cohesive purpose and (what seems to be) common sense of collecting and preserving films that exists today did not take root in the public imagination until the 1980s. This chapter reveals that early advocates' rhetoric did not necessarily focus on the fact that the nation's filmic record was disintegrating, and there was not a widespread assumption that the moving image was an obvious bulwark to shoring up the past. While there was not a unified philosophy for preserving film in the early years of cinema collecting and archiving, there was a nationalistic undercurrent that ran through much of the early film collection rhetoric. To some extent this is because the collection advocates were attempting to create national collections and because many collectors believed the cinema had the potential to help shape the United States' cultural, aesthetic, and political identity. Firmly ensconced in popular culture by the 1930s and 1940s, cinema and its amassing seemed to be the perfect solution to disparate concerns and fears during an era when the United States was coming into its own as a global giant. Many early collectors and archivists believed that film collections could ameliorate various institutional, cultural, and national anxieties. Less than a half of a century after its introduction, cinema had so permeated the cultural consciousness of the United States that culture industry leaders sought to use films as a vital and rhetorical tool for enhancing the reputation of the United States, both to its own citizens and to the rest of the world.

The Film Industry as Good Cultural Citizen

While the film industry's attitude has changed toward its care of older films in the last decade, archivists have routinely vilified the industry's disregard and neglect of its film collections. Studios have a history of throwing their products away, letting them disintegrate, and dumping them into archives without helping to pay for their care. Thus, it may come as some surprise that one of the first efforts to create a national film collection was initiated by Will H. Hays, president of the Motion Picture Producers and Distributors Association (MPPDA). Hired to run the association in 1921, Hays already had a long record as an administrator as a railroad executive, the chairman of the Republican Party, and President Warren G. Harding's Postmaster General in 1920. "Reflecting the corporate side of Progressivism, he believed in business and government cooperation," writes Lary May, "a persuasion that made him an ideal administrator well worth his $100,000 a year salary."[4] Hays worked diligently to build the film industry's public image as a good citizen and helped make it an orderly business with solid relationships with banks and the government. Hays regularly proclaimed that Hollywood film not only sold an American way of life but also its consumer products as well, and like other leaders in the industry worked to counteract Hollywood's reputation as a stronghold of moral corruption. Hays's purpose for securing films of historical importance, to be sure, was primarily aimed toward enhancing the film industry's reputation as a forthright cultural, commercial, and patriotic industry. His eleven-year effort lobbying for a national film collection launched a preservation campaign and brought popular attention to the idea that film artifacts were of historical importance.[5]

Hays's proposal, which began as a vision for a film vault in the basement of the White House did not came to fruition, but he did contribute to the 1930 architectural plan for the National Archives which included film vaults for storing films and sound recordings pertaining to and illustrating historical activities in the United States.[6] In 1923, Hays discussed the possibility of a film vault with President Harding who died before Hays's vision could be implemented. Five years after securing his position as the president of the MPPDA, Hays outlined a plan to President Calvin Coolidge for how preserving films would be vital to the education of future generations. Hays explained to President Coolidge that there were already plenty of important films to be stored in the government's vaults: William McKinley's inauguration, films made during Theodore Roosevelt's administration, the signing of the Versailles Treaty, the burying of the unknown soldier, the flying of the first air machine, the operation of the first wireless, and "pictures showing the costumes and habits of peoples, all of great interest in future periods."[7] Coolidge who seemed persuaded by Hays's proposal pondered what it might mean for the present generation if films of Abraham Lincoln's Gettysburg Address were available with "all its coloring and historical characters moving on the stage as in real life."[8]

Hays had some support for his national collection plan from the film industry, politicians, and academics. Shortly after Hays and Coolidge's meeting, an article in the *New York Times* explaining Hays's efforts, focused on the opinions of J. J. McCarthy, head of the Epoch Producing Company that held the rights to *The Birth of a Nation*. McCarthy surely held a potentially large personal and financial stake in Hays's plan, and of course the history lessons in *The Birth of a Nation* are dubious at best. Nonetheless, McCarthy spoke like a present-day archivist when he explained, "it is worth noting that not all history is contained in the textbooks, and that State gazetteers, archives and chronologies do not contain sufficient clues to the life of a period."[9] William Fox also jumped on the archival bandwagon as he announced he would donate a copy of the film *What Price Glory* to the Washington archive. Professors from both Yale and Columbia who had watched *What Price Glory* proclaimed its historic importance, adding support, it appeared, to Hays's proposal. Hays's plan even included exhibiting archival films on transatlantic ships to promote the virtues of American life to immigrants: "A communication from Mr. Hays's office says that patriotic and historical pictures are to be shown in the steerage of transatlantic vessels to immigrants. These films will be furnished free of charge, and will be specially selected so as to give the future Americans their first lesson in American citizenship."[10]

While it is likely that sea weary immigrants would have enjoyed such a cinematic distraction, Hays's implausible on-board citizenship lessons suggests how far he was willing to go to promote the film industry as a committed partner in the nation's well-being. Nonetheless, Hays's rhetoric had a powerful impact on the popular imagination. The Pulitzer Prize–winning writer Alva Johnston, a month after Hays's meeting with President Coolidge, likened the nine-hundred-year-old Bayeux tapestry to archived cinema, stating that the tapestry is "nothing more than a 231-foot news reel in needlework." Poking fun of cinema while praising Hays's efforts at the same time, Johnston wrote:

> The schoolboys of 3000 or 4000 A.D. may learn about us from the venerable news reels (*sic*) and dramas. Instead of reading corpulent

volumes of history, they will troop to the school movie houses to hoot their forefathers and write exercises on "The Slow Motion Era" and "Factors that Retarded the Development of the Early Twentieth Century Brain." Even so, it is pretty certain that distant ages will appreciate the courtesy of Mr. Hays and the motion picture industry in setting aside these films for them.[11]

Famous for his persuasive tactics, in-house censorship, and the Motion Picture Production Code, Hays is less remembered as an altruist or pioneer in film preservation, but he did bring attention to the burgeoning discourse about the historical worth of older films. The National Archives Act signed by President Franklin D. Roosevelt and passed by the 73rd Congress on June 19, 1934, included a provision for motion pictures and sound recordings, with acquisitions beginning in 1935. However, the National Archives Act did not help Hays and other motion picture industry leaders create a government-sponsored national film library that would house both industry and government films. Established as an independent agency of the executive branch, the National Archives was built for the purpose of maintaining the permanent records documenting the policies and activities of the federal government.

The Moving Image Artifact and Historical Truth

Modern historiography can be characterized, in part, by its effort to bridge the gap between the past and the present. In its effort to construct knowledge about a time period that it can never access, historiography privileges the authenticated primary source document. Shortly after cinema became popularized, people began considering the film image as an authentic historical document because the moving image camera is able to capture and preserve an occurrence in historical time. "Photography preserves an instant of time for a subject," Philip Rosen explains, "but cinema preserves a fragment of time that can be experienced as actual duration. Time itself seems captured."[12] It may seem obvious to the reader that the moving image has the uncanny ability to transport the viewer to a different time period; however, in the first decades of the twentieth century, people were just beginning to establish a rhetorical frame for film's significance to the historic record.

Not surprisingly, it was the people within the film industry who were the first to imagine how films might function as part of history. An editorial in the 1906 industry trade paper *Views and Film Index,* for example, suggested that in fifty or one hundred years films might become vital archival documents. The editorial acknowledged that the past disappears so quickly in a culture fixated on progress that photographs and film could help to prevent the obliteration of memory, suggesting that, "perhaps the day will come when motion pictures will be treasured by governments in their museums as vital documents in their historical archives."[13] The editorial urged readers to consider the cultural impact of film and its unique ability to record both everyday life and monumental events. Interestingly, films of such import included mundane scenes of city streets as well as the historic occasions of presidential gatherings. In this early view, motion pictures were envisioned as a time capsule that could cultivate cultural memory, affording future generations the ability to see a past that would presumably be wiped out by twentieth-century progress.

A 1915 editorial in *Motography* entitled "Can Films be Preserved for Posterity?" pointed to the potential problems that came with saving motion picture film; namely that its chemical properties and composition might lead to instability, flammability, and the growth of fungus. The editorial's concerns about film storage and chemical instability were driven by a desire to preserve moving images of the important scenes of World War I. "Now that the greatest event in world history is transpiring, so to speak, before our cameras," the editorial explained, "the historians are offered their first extraordinary opportunity to establish archives of film records, to preserve into the indefinite future *the exact replicas* of today's actions."[14] The editorial's archival impulse is, in part, driven by reports of the German government filming and archiving their participation in the war. It was also motivated by the possibility that future generations could be imbued with patriotism if they were afforded the chance to see "the exact replicas of today's actions." Both the 1906 and 1915 editorials suggested that films should be collected for future generations because they were documents of significant human activity. If films were protected, both editorials reasoned, future generations would have access to history and consequently be moved to patriotism. Such early inclinations toward preservation were centered on the nonfictional moving images that could offer future generations ways to see history in the making.

John G. Bradley and R.D.W Connor at the National Archives were instrumental in institutionalizing the moving image as part of the historic record. Bradley, who was the clerk of the Joint Committee on the Library in 1933–34, appointed the first Archivist of the United States, R.D.W. Connor, a history professor at the University of North Carolina. Connor in turn appointed Bradley as the first chief of Motion Pictures and Sound Recordings at the National Archives. While their relationship appears self-serving, Connor was a well-respected historian who had served as the North Carolina Archivist prior to his appointment as first Archivist of the United States. He and Bradley helped to advance the relationship between moving images and history and helped to cultivate the rhetoric for moving images as a respected artifact. As stated earlier, Hays's proposal for a national collection was not realized, but when Roosevelt signed the National Archives Act on June 19, 1934, a provision for motion pictures and sound recordings was included. Established as an independent agency of the executive branch, the National Archives was established for the purpose of maintaining the permanent records documenting the policies and activities of the Federal Government. Section 7 of the National Archives Act did specifically address audio-visual documents. It reads, "The National Archives may also accept, store, and preserve motion-picture films and sound recordings pertaining to and illustrative of historical activities of the United States, and in connection therewith maintain a projecting room for showing such films and reproducing such sound recordings for historical purposes and study."

While Section 7 stated that the National Archives could accept motion picture films, the National Archives Act in general established a National Archives of the *United States Government*. The inclusion of motion pictures and sound recordings as archival materials in the 1934 act, according to the National Archives historian Marjorie H. Ciarlante, was visionary. Written during a time when "virtually no other archival institution addressed itself to the preservation of motion pictures and sound recordings as permanently valuable historical documents," the eventual development of the Motion Pictures and Sound Recordings Division helped to establish and promote the belief that motion pictures had enough cultural and historic value for the U.S. government to protect them.[15] The act also helped to place motion pictures in a new category: objects of archival interest.

Section 7's lack of specificity regarding the kinds of films that could be collected at the National Archives opened the door for Bradley, the first head of the Motion Pictures and Sound Recordings Division, to have a broader interpretation of what sorts of motion pictures and sound recordings could be accepted. The language of section 7 enabled Bradley to have a somewhat liberal collection policy. According to Ciarlante, the Motion Pictures and Sound Recordings Division had a more inclusive collection than that of the rest of the National Archives. "What Bradley did, in a word, was to broaden the definition of 'United States history' to an all-inclusive term," Ciarlante explained, "'reflection of the American scene,' to encompass all fields of human endeavor with 'virtually nothing excluded.' By so doing, he reopened the issue of the original intent of the law; i.e., 'history of the U.S. Government' versus 'U.S. history in its broadest sense,' an issue upon which he refused to compromise and which ultimately forced his resignation from the National Archives."[16] In 1945, Bradley was appointed director of the Motion Picture Division at the Library of Congress and retired from the government three years later.

In a 1935 *New York Times* editorial, Connor noted the provision for motion pictures and sound recordings in the 1934 National Archives Act had piqued considerable public interest. He proclaimed that the motion picture provision was "one of the most important activities of the National Archives Establishment." Furthermore, Connor explained that films, vaults, and projection room, are for the purpose of historical study; the films would not be available for the general public. Issues of moving image accessibility would not arise until much later in the twentieth century. "The possibilities which motion pictures and sound recordings open up for the future historian," he said, "are boundless," and these helped to establish their significance, their seriousness, as archival artifacts in the popular imagination.[17] Perhaps his most radical message was his argument in the popular press that future historians would learn truths about the history of the United States by watching motion pictures, specifically those housed in the National Archives. Because the film industry that had pushed for a national film collection was not willing to help fund it and because the Great Depression budget was too slight to construct a building to store the films, the original intent for a national film collection was not realized.

It is likely that the National Archives has turned away more film footage than it has acquired over the years due to space and economic constraints. Its collection consists primarily of film and video materials from all government agencies, including newsreels, television newscasts, and coverage of congressional committee hearings. Because government film footage is in the public domain, the National Archives is a popular, accessible, and inexpensive source for stock footage. On any given day, hordes of filmmakers and researchers access the more than 300,000 reels of motion picture holdings at the Motion Picture, Sound, and Video unit in College Park, Maryland. Surely, Bradley and Connor would be satisfied to know that at least part of their vision for motion pictures has been realized.

Copyright and Collecting

The Film Library at the Museum of Modern Art and the Motion Pictures and Sound Recordings Division at the National Archives were the primary institutions, prior to the 1940s, that promoted the collection and preservation of films and endorsed the idea that older films were useful tools for intellectual inquiry. But when Archibald MacLeish was appointed as the Librarian of Congress in October 1939, he made a series of decisions that helped to put motion pictures collecting on the map at the Library of Congress. MacLeish envisioned and then initiated a plan to create a national film collection at the Library of Congress. He helped to initiate five different strategies in order for the national film collection to be realized. MacLeish restored the original conditions of the motion picture copyright deposit;[18] he supported the transfer of the recently recovered paper print collection to celluloid; he promoted the private donations of films made during the thirty year period from 1912–42 when the library did not collect motion pictures; he created a collaboration between MoMA and the Library of Congress by which a committee selected the most significant films made each year; and he created a Motion Picture Division at the Library of Congress.

MacLeish's reorganization of the Library of Congress brought forth its revitalization, but more important for our purposes, it led to the rediscovery of the paper print collection in 1940. Probably the most significant early film collection in the United States was collected quite by accident as a result of early film companies attempting to ward off piracy and bootlegging. This collection of early motion pictures was actually contact copies of film on paper, originally submitted to the library for copyright protection. The paper print collection, created as a result of a copyright law of 1870, is an important chapter in the United States history of film preservation, and it is important and interesting enough to outline it in some detail here.

One of MacLeish's first tasks as the Librarian of Congress was to confront the overwhelming backlog of material, more than one million and one-half books, left by his predecessors Ainsworth Rand Spofford, John Russell Young, and Herbert Putnam. In MacLeish's efforts to deal with this overwhelming task, he reorganized the library's thirty-five divisions into five departments: Processing, Reference, Administration, Law Library, and the Copyright Offices. From the beginning of his tenure as the Librarian of Congress in 1864, Ainsworth Spofford lobbied for a revision of the copyright law so to help build a national library at the Library of Congress. In 1870, the law was changed to read: "all records and other things relating to copyrights and required by law to be preserved shall be under the control of the Librarian of Congress."[19] After the law was passed, a vast amount of material was added to the library collection. Doug Herrick explains that Spofford "cast his net wide" in his quest for books for his national collection. "Soon LC found itself reeling," Herrick writes, "under a torrent of maps, charts, manuscripts, sheet music, prints, lithographs, engravings, photographs, and motion pictures."[20] While the 1870 law opened the gates for nonprint material to be collected at the Library of Congress, it was not until 1912 that copyright laws actually protected motion pictures.

With no protection, there were rampant problems for film producers as well as literary authors whose works were routinely made into motion pictures without permission or compensation. "Copyright infringement litigation, suits, and countersuits were the order of the day," writes Herrick. "One of the main problems was that the copyright law up to 1912 continued not to recognize motion pictures during a period when the medium was becoming less an eccentric novelty and more a big business."[21] A 1911 Supreme Court case (Kalem Co. v. Harper Bros., 222 U.S. 55) brought an end to motion picture producers making films from literary works without consent or compensation. With the 1912 passage of the Townsend Act, motion pictures were recognized as entities deserving of copyright protection.

Because the Library of Congress did not have a provision for motion picture registration during the earliest years of the motion picture industry, early film movie companies who wished to protect their motion pictures from piracy and bootlegging cleverly deposited their films for copyright protections on paper strips. These strips were, in essence, photographic paper reels. This process of donating paper copies of films enabled motion picture companies such as Edison, Biograph, and Méliès to have copyright protection because there were such provisions in place for photographs. From 1897 until 1917, film companies deposited paper reels to the library; the paper strips (that could not be projected) were stored like all other copyright records.

When MacLeish reorganized the library, part of the task of the Copyright Office was to reconstitute its own files. As a result of this process the paper prints were uncovered in an old vault in the south cellar of the Main Building in the summer of 1942. Uncovering the paper reels revealed the earliest chapter in motion picture history. Five thousand film subjects and approximately two and one-half million feet of paper film had been stored away at the library. Since they were copied on paper, rather than nitrate film, they had not decomposed. Charles Grimm has suggested that some longtime library employees knew about the paper strips, but viewed them as mere registration material and did not consider them to have historic value.[22] Howard Walls, a copyright clerk, was at least partially responsible for the discovery of the paper prints and was instrumental in framing their recovery in a way that suggested that the Library of Congress now had virtually all of the beginnings of American cinema. MacLeish, in his 1942 *Annual Report of the Librarian of Congress,* noted the discovery of the paper prints stating that they "cannot take the place of the missing films, but they constitute, nevertheless, a basis on which a collection of value and importance can now be made."[23]

Less than a year later, in May 1943, Walls, who was then no longer a copyright clerk but was in charge of Motion Pictures Collections at the library, presented a talk "Motion Picture Incunabula in the Library of Congress" to the Society of Motion Picture Engineers. During his talk Walls explained that a cooperative effort with the National Archives, motion picture engineer Carol Louis Gregory had developed a process to transfer the paper prints to celluloid. Walls proclaimed that with this discovery, the early history of cinema would no longer be left to conjecture. The Library of Congress now had evidence of the beginnings of the motion picture history of the United States—at least the early record of copyrighted cinema. The paper prints not only provided a record of early cinematic history, it also offered a *view* of early twentieth century history. Walls explained, "For the first time, the complete and analytical history of the early motion picture may be written without resort to conjecture, and The Library of Congress is in a position to provide graphic and lifelike information concerning notable personages of the past, historical events, and the customs and mores of a bygone and captivating era."[24]

Two days after Walls's speech, the *New York Times* weighed in on the meaning of the paper prints. The editorial is revealing, for it offers the popular view of older films in 1943. The editorial begins by explaining that the five thousand films will be restored for "those who care to see them." It concludes with an evaluation of their cultural value. "The youngsters who throng Times Square to listen to the latest trumpet tooter would not cross the street to see them; or if they did would jeer where their father and grandfathers wept bitter tears," the editorial reads. "Films of long-past years are not good by anybody's standards. They were good, however, for their day."[25] Old films, according to the editorial, were not for viewing because their sentiment and technology were not sophisticated enough for modern tastes, but they were important enough to keep around because they represented the origins of the cinematic art form. The editorial did not mention, as Walls had, that the films were also visual artifacts providing a keyhole view of history, suggesting that while Bradley and Connor had initiated critical discourse in the 1930s, a decade later motion pictures still did not have cultural cache as historic evidence by the mainstream press.

Walls's response to the editorial was published as a letter to the editor of the *New York Times* on May 20. Walls thanked the *Times* for responding favorably to the library's plan to restore the paper prints, but hastened to add that while the fictional films of the collection were significant to scholars of "cinematic growth," it was the nonfiction films that were of the greatest value within the collection. Walls stated the nonfiction films in the paper print collection could bring history to life "far more forcibly than the printed word or the still photograph." He concluded his letter to the editor by explaining that the collection will appeal to historians, educators, and sociologists, even if they have "no interest in the motion picture as such."[26] Walls's comments are representative of the bifurcated view of the significance of older films prior to the 1980s. Most champions of archival film imagined that they were useful tools for either the social historian or the cinema scholar, but rarely both.

The paper print transfer and the collaboration between the National Archives and the Library of Congress did not proceed smoothly. Among other factors, World War II intervened, and in August 1947, the library announced that it was liquidating its motion picture project because Congress had not supplied funds for its operation.[27] In 1949, the Library of Congress and National Archives terminated their joint projects and the paper prints were once again put into storage. Nonetheless, the paper print discovery and the technological developments for their transfer were important incidents in the burgeoning years of film preservation in the United States. When motion pictures were beginning to gain recognition as culturally significant, the discovery of the paper print collection provided the basis for the cinematic Genesis story. Its foundational value offered validation to both the cinema and film scholar, who until the discovery had "done well with the material at his disposal," Walls explained, "but he has been denied access to the great body of material which would have broadened his scope and placed him upon paths leading to greater truths."[28]

Walls continued to have a relationship with the paper print collection after he left Washington, D.C. Hired at the Academy of Motion Picture Arts and Sciences to build the film collection, he also was given the task to transfer the paper prints to film. With an extremely small budget, Walls had a difficult time accomplishing what he had set out to do and was ultimately fired. However, the paper prints were not forgotten. Hired by AMPAS to locate some of the collection that were thought to be stolen but were actually only misplaced (it is probably the only major film collection that has supposedly been misplaced twice in its history), ex-Los Angeles policeman, deputy, and one-time Howard Hughes bodyguard Kemp Niver ultimately created a machine that could transfer the paper to 16 mm film (Walls had transferred the prints to 35 mm). Niver, who received an honorary Academy Award in 1956 for the development of the machine, which he called the Ronovare Process, transferred about one-third of the paper print titles. Niver's work was initially funded by AMPAS and then by congressional appropriation, but in 1958, the Library of Congress received a congressional appropriation to finish the transfers and the library was in the motion picture business once again. The Stack and Reader Division at the library began working on the paper print transfers as well as other preservation projects in 1958, and the library's relationship with motion pictures has remained steadfast since then. The Library of Congress created the Motion Pictures, Broadcasting, and Recorded Sound Division in 1979, which as we will see in the chapters that follow, was the same period that the cultural significance of moving images as something more than entertainment began to permeate the public imagination.

The Moving Image Artifact as Film History

As we have seen, many of the efforts to collect film during the first half of the twentieth century focused on moving images' ability to transcend temporality and to portray historic events in a way that seemed uncannily lifelike. Valued as a historian's tool, collectors did not focus their attention on the importance of the medium itself but instead concentrated on what moving images might convey in the future. However, in the mid-1930s, at the same time that the National Archives began acquiring moving images, the British-born Iris Barry, the first curator of the Museum of Modern Art Film Library, played a major role in creating a film collection that shifted America's attitudes toward film.[29] Barry created a collection that was focused on the origins of cinema itself, a new art and technological form whose beginnings could be easily traced. Barry's rhetoric often included an underpinning of nationalism; the United States in the 1930s was anxious about Europe's cultural superiority, but cinema, Barry suggested, could ease such anxiety if it was rightfully placed (and consequently valued) in the museum. For our purposes, one of Barry's largest contributions was her keen ability to explain how a viewer should watch an older film. While Bradley, Connor, Walls, and even Hays contributed to the rhetoric of why older films mattered and should be collected, Barry carefully and clearly explicated that they should actually be viewed once they were part of a collection.

The Museum of Modern Art, in 1935, announced that it had established its Film Library so that film could be studied as art. The museum had opened only six years earlier on November 7, 1929, ten days after the stock market crash. Its first director, Alfred Barr, had a collecting vision that clashed with the museum's earliest trustees' traditional and Eurocentric values. Rather than focusing only on painting and sculpture, Barr integrated prints, drawings, architecture, commercial art, industrial art, movies, theater design, and photography. "Integrating this perspective with the challenges of modern art in modern times," Haidee Wasson explains, "Barr's concept of art history entailed a vast and complex movement whose products could be found across political and national borders, across identifiable aesthetic movements and, crucially, among the complex interactions of the machine and the human."[30] Under Barr's reign, MoMA aimed to become a "national educational institution, committed to making art and museums an integral aspect of daily life, exploring the aesthetic of the profound as well as the prosaic," Wasson writes.[31] Barr aimed to integrate the museum into everyday life and incorporate everyday life into the museum; thus, it cannot be a surprise that six years after its inception MoMA announced the establishment of the Film Library.

In a report submitted to the Rockefeller Foundation for potential funding, MoMA constructed the argument for why an American film library was necessary. Authored by Barry and her husband John E. Abbott, the report indicated the library would "trace, catalogue, assemble, exhibit, and circulate to museums and colleges single films or programmes of films in exactly the same manner in which the Museum traces, catalogues, exhibits, and circulates paintings, sculpture, architectural photographs and models or reproductions of works of art, so that the film may be studied and enjoyed as any other of the arts is studied and enjoyed."[32] In May 1935, one month after they received the report, the Rockefeller Foundation informed MoMA of their intention to fund the Film Library. Barr and Abbott's argument for the library focused on three innovative views: film was art; film should be considered and treated in the exact manner as other, more traditional art forms; and like other arts, it was a cultural form worthy of *study*. The Film Library's aim was to collect and preserve motion pictures so to make them available to colleges and museums; two institutions that could and would ultimately give film cultural credibility. A year after the Film Library's inception, Barry happily wrote that "an increasing number of American universities and colleges, as well as adult education groups in many cities, are thus enabled to undertake for the first time a serious and critical study of this new omnipotent medium."[33]

If the MoMA Film Library was to promote the study of film, it was necessary to have a film collection, a body of work, from which to draw. Barry and her husband traveled to Hollywood and across Europe to collect films for the library. For the most part, Barry and Abbott had little immediate success securing films during their visit to Hollywood. But Mary Pickford did hold a reception for them at Pickfair and during the reception Barry held a film screening for the attendees. It was one of the first of many occasions that Barry would publicly educate and shape the way people understood film and its past. The clips, projected in chronological order ranged from *The Great Train Robbery* (1903, Edison Porter), to *The New York Hat* (1912, Biograph), to *Pluto's Judgment Day* (1935, Disney). Some of the film choices were obvious: Pickford, the hostess, starred in *The New York Hat.* The *Great Train Robbery,* according to Barry, was a demonstration of film's "first stumblings upon genuinely cinematic narration."[34] But the addition of the new Disney film at the Pickfair reception is, perhaps, more difficult to understand. Barry seems to have been the master of cinematic *inclusion* in order to meet the Film Library's collecting goals. Wasson argues that from its inception, the library served as a site of negotiation and compromise. While its ultimate aim was to elevate film to art form on the same level as sculpture and painting, in order to obtain a film collection for study, the library staff had to use "the term 'art' rather loosely." Wasson writes, "more often than not it was subsumed by a historical and educational discourse geared towards celebrating the industry."[35]

Barry's first trip to Hollywood was not particularly successful. Part of the problem was that the recently established Museum of Modern Art and the Film Library did not have enough cultural power to draw substantial interest in Hollywood. Studio heads conceived of the value in older films as profit potential only, and some were uneasy about their films being labeled as "art." As Barry later recognized, the power to acquire films for the Film Library lay not in Hollywood, but with New York studio lawyers. "It was however the corporation lawyers of Metro-Goldwyn-Mayer, Robert Rubin, back in New York, who finally drew up the contract—a tough one—governing the Film Library's acquisition and use of films," Barry wrote.[36] Barry negotiated the first North American legal definition of nonprofit feature film exhibition. Once a film had a two-year period of being commercially viable, a film, after negotiation, could enter the archive and be exhibited for educational and nonprofit purposes.[37] Once the Film Library began acquiring films, Barry and her staff studied the incoming films and then organized film study programs for educational institutions. Their first educational series, composed in part by the films that she had been able to collect, was entitled A Short Survey of the Film in America, 1894–1932. The survey consisted of five different programs: "The Development of the

Narrative," "The Rise of the American Film," "D. W. Griffith," "The German Influence," and "The Talkies." For institutions that did not have sound equipment, the Film Library organized a program entitled "The End of the Silent Era." Barry wrote in the summer of 1936, "Since January 1st of this year, our film programmes have been loaned to 72 colleges and societies and the popularity of the Library is steadily growing."[38]

Barry was self-conscious of the task she was undertaking; she understood that to collect, study, and analyze the beginnings of the art of film was an endeavor of tremendous proportions. "It will be the first time in history that any such first-hand record of the birth of a new art will have been undertaken: we ourselves in the Film Library have merely the first students in this field" wrote Barry. "And, most encouraging and most helpful, our researches are really proving successful largely because—far from being solitary workers—we represent only the American wing of a spontaneous and universal movement to preserve a record of the birth and development of the art of the cinema."[39]

But Barry's reasons for collecting and studying films varied according to her audience and the time period in which she was writing. In 1969, she remembered that a determining factor in the initial formation of the Film Library was the overwhelmingly affirmative response to a letter she had sent to heads of educational institutions inquiring if they would welcome a series of programs.

She explained to a Hollywood industry audience in 1946 why old films should be dragged back into the light. She reasoned that it benefited the esteem and standing of the motion picture industry because if the films of the past are significant enough for study, contemporary films must be worthy of analysis as well. Collecting and studying old films also enabled those involved in the film industry to learn from the past. "The opportunity to refer again to the more important films of the past," Barry explained, "must surely serve the same purpose as a library of books serves a writer."[40] Barry also cited the importance of the pleasure in seeing the older films and the significance of observing what original "flappers," "vamps," and "bright young people" looked like. Most important, Barry explained, the value of older films was important for contemporary technicians. Much could be learned by seeing the camerawork, the editing, the directing, and by listening to the use of sound and music in older films. Barry concludes the article with an appeal. "Now is the time for Hollywood and its technicians to join the Film Library in a collaboration that would once and for all give precise information to students everywhere about the styles and innovations, the creative contributions, of the men and women working in motion pictures everywhere in the world for the past fifty years—the achievements that have carried the motion picture from its celebrated infancy to near maturity and made it indeed an art (as well as an industry) with which one can truly be proud to be connected."[41]

Appealing to an academic audience, Barry stressed that the Film Library's collection was for the purpose of constructing a record of the development of cinematic art by the way of "first-hand examinations."[42] In the same year that she published her plea to help construct a historical record of the industry's achievements in *Hollywood Quarterly*, she argued in *College Art Journal* that there was as of yet insufficient scholarship focusing on film history and aesthetics. Since the founding of the Film Library, Barry explained, "a much keener interest in the sociological implications of the motion picture has been elicited than its aesthetic content, and it would be unfortunate if this unbalance were to persist."[43] Barry not only encouraged researchers to take the study of the film itself seriously, she provided a lengthy list of research questions for the potential film scholar. Focusing on issues concerning film editing, style, theme, and genre, Barry exclaimed the realm of inquiry was endless. Perhaps most important, Barry explains that the Film Library has created an environment where such research is possible because she and her staff had collected films for the library, and the materiality of the films made serious study possible.

Cinematic scholarship, as Barry defined it, required the expert's eye directly encountering the images on the screen. Memory was not enough. Of course, her focus on observation corresponded with the museum's policy and obligation toward displaying its collections.[44] Barry's influence on cinematic culture was profound, as she shaped the way film itself was understood. But her lessons about watching film were also pragmatic for the archive. Instructing a generation to look at and make sense of a film once it was placed in a collection, Barry refined the meaning of the moving image archive. She gave it clear purpose and a well-defined identity. Under Barry's instruction, the moving image archive became a scholarly site of investigation, rather than just a place where old films were kept.

One Must Play the Historian Oneself, and Precociously

MacLeish's focus on motion pictures during his tenure as the Librarian of Congress altered the library's relationship with motion pictures and helped to push the cultural significance of films and their preservation into a brighter light. A poet, playwright, and political activist, MacLeish was an early advocate of the United States involvement in the war. His view of motion pictures at the Library of Congress was shaped by both his political views and the fact that he became the librarian a month after World War II broke out in 1939. During his tenure (1939–44) as Librarian of Congress, he held other important governmental offices that also shaped his perception of the role of motion pictures at the library. Before the Pearl Harbor attack in 1941, President Roosevelt asked MacLeish to head the Office of Facts and Figures. He then became the assistant director of Office of War Information (OWI) in 1942.

As the assistant director of the OWI, MacLeish was part of a team that worked to mobilize positive images of the United States to an international audience. President Roosevelt issued Executive Order no. 9182, creating the OWI in June 1942. An autonomous agency, the OWI absorbed the functions of the Office of Facts and Figures, the Office of Government Reports, the division of information at the Office for Emergency Management, and the foreign information service at the Coordinator of Information. The OWI coordinated the release of war news for domestic use and launched a propaganda campaign abroad. During the early 1940s policymakers believed that the image the United States projected abroad was critical to the country's foreign policy. The "United States could best advance its own geopolitical position through selling its ideology and its way of life," Justin Hart writes, "rather than through costly and disruptive exercises in military conquest. Simply put, Americanization became the antidote to colonization."[45] Hart contends that the OWI became the first governmental agency to "be assigned custodial responsibility for the nation's overall image in the world."[46]

The Bureau of Motion Pictures (BMP) in the OWI acted as the intermediary between federal agencies and the radio and motion picture industries. The BMP wrote a manual entitled *Government Information Manual for the Motion Picture Industry* in 1942. A comprehensive portrait of the bureau's interpretation of the war, the manual explained the ideology of the OWI and directed the film industry to produce films that appropriately promoted its principles. The BMP distributed weekly additions to the loose-leaf manual so to keep the movie industry continually updated. Hollywood was, in effect, charged with representing American democratic ideals and the practicalities of fighting a war. While the manual consistently urged Hollywood to make films that constituted the abstract notions of American determination and goodness, it also offered Hollywood ways to practically represent and aid the war effort.

The BMP suggested what should be portrayed on screen, and it also voiced its approval or disapproval of films being distributed. One particular film of 1942, of which the BMP approved for example, was *Casablanca*. As historians Clayton Koppes and Gregory Black explain, the BMP liked the 1942 Academy Award winner because of its "depiction of the valiant underground, the United States as the haven of the oppressed, and subordination of personal desires to the greater cause of the war—although they would have preferred that the hero had verbalized the reasons for his conversion."[47] The overarching effects of the BMP on the film industry should not be underestimated. "From mid-1943 until the end of the war, OWI exerted an influence over an American mass medium never equaled before or since by a government agency," write Koppes and Black. "The content of World War II motion pictures is inexplicable without reference to the bureau."[48]

Such an overt push to regulate the circulation of moving images in Hollywood suggests that MacLeish's drive for a national film collection at the Library of Congress was partially motivated by World War II, his participation with the OWI, and the effort by the OWI to disseminate positive views of America. In the 1942 *Annual Report of the Librarian of Congress* MacLeish explained that a new procedure regarding the selection of motion pictures for the library's collection was brought along to some extent by the ongoing war. MacLeish stated that the war "emphasized the tremendous historical and scholarly importance of much current film."[49] In order to develop the national collection, the Library of Congress, the Museum of Modern Art Film Library, and the Rockefeller Foundation agreed upon an arrangement whereby the staff at the Film Library selected and stored the films released during the calendar year. The criteria for selecting the films was developed by MacLeish, his friend Robert Penn Warren, Iris Barry, John Abbott, and others at the Film Library. In 1942, the first year of the agreement, MoMA received $25,000 from the Rockefeller Foundation to pay staff to screen American motion pictures deposited for copyright and then select the appropriate films for preservation. The selected films were then stored in vaults rented by the Museum of Modern Art.

During the first year of the film selection process the selection committee chose 104 films released in 1942. According to MacLeish, in his 1943 *Report of the Librarian of Congress*, the criteria for selection were based on "those films which will provide future students with the most truthful and revealing information the cinema can provide as to the life and interests of the men and women of the period." He specifically stated five categories of greatest interest: newsreels and news-related films of probable interest to students of the time; documentary films of probable interest to the social historian and political historian; films that mark important artistic and technological advances in the art of motion pictures; films such as certain animated cartoons that reveal the imaginative life of the period; and outstanding scientific and geographic films. Many of the films are newsreels and documentaries directly related to the war effort. The documentaries that dominate the list could best be described as extended newsreels about the war: *The Fighting French; Beyond the Line of Duty; The Price of Victory; Prelude to Victory;* and *Inside Fascist Spain.* Nearly all of the fictional films' plots deal directly with World War II. Films such as *Mrs. Miniver; Wake Island; In Which We Serve; The War Against Mrs. Hadley;* and *This Land is Mine* strongly suggest that the selection process for the national film collection at the Library of Congress was aimed to effectively aid the war effort.

The process for selecting the 1942 films was detailed in an article published in *The Library of Congress Quarterly Journal.* The author, Barbara Deming, who would later become a well-known peace activist during the 1960s, was a member of the selection committee. Deming and her colleagues Norbert Lusk, Philip Hartung, Liane Richter, and Barbara Symmes screened 1,400 motion pictures and narrowed the selection down to 104 films for the national collection. The general principle guiding the selection process, Deming explains, is to serve the student of history rather than the cinema scholar. Deming outlines the system of analysis that the committee employed for determining the films most appropriate for the national collection. Deming's article explicates the method the selection committee used for choosing films that would be of service to future historians.

The selection committee's analysis was based on criteria borrowed from Siegfried Kracauer's developing theory of film. Deming acknowledges a "friendly debt" to Kracauer, the German film theorist who worked at the Museum of Modern Art after he immigrated to the United States in 1941. A contemporary of Walter Benjamin's, Kracauer believed that there was a correspondence between the basic properties of film and the underlying properties of modernity.

Deming places films in two categories: direct and indirect mode. Films either confront the zeitgeist literally and directly or they portray the times by representation, reflecting the mentality of a period. Fictional films of the direct mode, Deming argues, are mirrors of the period and reveal the details of daily life and the material truths of a period. The historian can discern the spirit of an age by observing clothing, the props of daily life, language use, and even the ways in which actors sing and dance. But the realities of social antipathy might also be revealed inadvertently, for Deming argues that it is often the filmmakers' naïveté rather than their sophistication that allows us to see the truth. "The makers will arrange the agreeable cliché at the surface, and then will be able without flinching to report all along the way the most unpleasant facts."[50]

Deming's account of the interpretive process of the films of the direct mode is generally straightforward and the selection process of these films surely aligned with MacLeish's desire to collect films that assisted the war effort. Her account of the significance of the films of the indirect mode, however, is more complex. Deming states that interpreting films in the indirect mode requires the analyst to step through the looking glass so to understand the psychology responsible for the film. Films of the indirect mode, she asserts, may service future historians by enabling them to see the culture's daydreams; films that reveal attitudes and beliefs not talked about but that are "felt in the bones." "Films will again and again, as dreams will, approach the same guilt feeling, trying to erase it, or approach the same anxiety, trying to relieve it, the same yen, trying to indulge it," Deming writes. "After examining the films of a period it is possible to constellate them finally in shifting groups about certain major pressure points."[51]

The selection committee's detailed and analytical approach to choosing the films reveals that the committee aimed to create a collection that both fulfilled the immediate needs of wartime while also preserving the World War II zeitgeist for future researchers. But their systematic approach did not prevent conflicts among the selection committee that were often resolved by way of Barry overriding the committee's decisions at the end of the deliberation process. MacLeish and Barry did not always agree on films because they came to the project with different collecting philosophies and with different audiences in mind. Barry, for example, rejected the Technicolor version of *For Whom the Bell Tolls* (Sam Wood, 1943) because she felt it was a bad version of Ernest Hemingway's novel. MacLeish, in this case, overturned her decision. "I am against you on *For Whom the Bell Tolls*," MacLeish wrote in a telegram to Barry, "not because I disagree with your statement, but because the film, bad as it was, throws a good deal of light on the state of the American mind during the war."[52] MacLeish and Barry's conflicts, as Peter Decherney explains, were largely a result of differing collecting principles and intentions at the institutions they represented:

> MoMA's staff selectively curated shows for immediate political purposes and released the programs to schools, museums, and film societies. The Library of Congress's collection was meant to be a time capsule, perfectly representative of the moment. But both were meant to be propaganda. MoMA's shows were designed to persuade audiences of the dominance of American culture; the LOC's collection was meant to control the conclusions of future historians about that culture.[53]

Deming and the rest of the selection committee completed the screening process at the end of April 1945. By the time they were finished, they had screened 4,398 films and had added 969 reels of film to the collection. The fact that the committee viewed, analyzed, and sifted through such a tremendous amount of films in such a short amount of time is a notable feat and an event that foreshadows the overwhelming abundance of material that present-day archivists routinely confront. Film collecting philosophies in contemporary archives are rarely as detailed as the selection committee's; however, the selection process for film preservation (within individual archives or for national efforts such as the National Film Registry) is a complicated one that is often tangled up in economics, politics, and minor culture wars. Deming freely admitted that the selection committee utilized a certain degree of guesswork. "This man rather than that man, this speech rather than that speech, will go down in history," Deming explains. "One must, in other words, play the historian oneself, and precociously."[54]

Present-day archivists who are careful not to identify themselves as historians would be averse to uttering much less publishing a statement such as Deming's. They often define themselves as the historian's handmaiden: collecting, cataloging, and preparing moving images for the historian who will eventually come along and make sense of films' meanings. But each archival choice—this film (rather than that film) collected, clearly cataloged, and preserved certainly shapes cinematic history. And choices necessarily must be made because of tight budgets and the profusion of archival materials. Today the organization or the individual that grants money for preservation work often shapes the preservation criteria. How and why a film is preserved becomes part of a film's biography. Archivists, who document the process like Deming did, serve cinema history well. Researchers should have access to information that enables them to understand why "this film rather than that film" was considered important enough to preserve during a particular historical period.

Like many of the attempts at a national film collection, the Library of Congress Film Project eventually collapsed. In 1947, the Republican Congress cut the wartime budget and the Motion Pictures Division was shut down. The Film Project was the last time that the Library of Congress had a particular collecting mission for moving images, though its identity was certainly shaped by way of the American Film Institute in 1968, as we shall see in the following chapter. Today it holds the largest collection of films in the United States mostly due to copyright deposits and its acquisition of many major and minor film collections. The Museum of Modern Art's Film Library eventually turned away from its sociological and psychological interests during the war and returned to its original collecting intentions of Hollywood films and Hollywood's major players.

Conclusion

The major developments that shaped the culture of the United States film archive during the thirties and forties came to a halt by the end of the 1940s. Relatively few archival initiatives took hold at the national level until the development of the American Film Institute in the 1960s, when the cultivation of a national film collection was considered a necessary weapon during the Cold War. The first attempts at creating national collections were instrumental in helping to bring value to cinema, Hollywood, and the nation during the first half of the twentieth century. The early promoters of film archiving were obviously farsighted, for they advocated for a visual historical record at the same time that the United States was growing into an image-based culture. In general, their vision was one in which the meanings of the collections were controlled and controllable, for many of the early film collections were meant to demonstrate the cultural, aesthetic, and political power of the United States to its own citizens and the rest of the world. The early rhetoric that placed high value on cinema as a significant historical artifact and an object of scholarly study has been sustained into the early twenty-first century. However, the nationalistic discourse that helped to shape early film collections has significantly diminished. The meanings of the film archive became less and less controllable as the twentieth century progressed, helping to liberate the archive from its original inclinations toward historicism and its nationalistic underpinnings.

In the first decade of the twenty-first century, the notion of a national collection situated within one archive is unfathomable. Today, there are simply far too many films (in part because there is an additional seventy years of filmmaking), collections, and archival interests for a national collection to be held under one institutional "roof." While Hollywood films and newsreels were once the primary archival focus, today amateur, technical, corporate, regional, avant-garde, experimental, and orphan films, along with home movies, short subjects, television movies, documentaries, and music videos are collected and preserved alongside more traditional archival interests. Today's archival culture seeks to collect and preserve films that are significant to the United States, but there is not a "one size fits all" archival collection. The dramatic increase in archives, archivists, and moving image collections, the professionalization of the archive, the popularization of cinema studies, and cultural workers' increasing distrust of narratives that claim to speak for and to an entire nation helped to construct multifarious archival collections that serve the fragmented and disparate interests of individuals and interest groups around the country and the world.[55]

2

ACCESSIBILITY, AUTHENTICITY, AND ANXIETY

When you ask a moving image archivist about YouTube, do not expect her to immediately exclaim its virtues as the twenty-first century town square. Do not think that she is going to straight away do a song-and-dance number for you about YouTube's democratization of the moving image. For many film archivists, YouTube (and other hosting/streaming sites) is a conundrum that highlights present-day archival anxieties about technology and the liberation of moving images from a controlled context. While YouTube enables users to exhibit and view a mind-boggling amount of moving images, it is also a site where image manipulation reigns supreme. Content providers routinely re-edit and re-cut and add new soundtracks to films, giving moving images new and altered meanings, divorced from their original context. For example, the user drkatzjr27 edited the scene from the film *Annie Hall* where Marshall McLuhan chastises a professor standing in a movie line. The original scene, according to drkatzjr27, is too long, so he shortened it to punctuate the scene's humor. "What a classic moment in film!" drkatzjr27 exclaims, as he modifies the very scene he is celebrating. For the archive to be relevant in our consumer culture, its holdings must be widely accessible, but accessibility is beholden to innovative technologies that also have the means to sever the moving image from the archive. This complex relationship between commercialization, technology, and accessibility began in earnest during the 1960s and has been instrumental in defining the parameters of the film archive ever since.

Many archivists find YouTube's ability to provide free and instant accessibility to massive amounts of moving images quite enviable. Some archival institutions, such as Northeast Historic Film (NHF), take advantage of YouTube's popularity and instant accessibility and post collection materials on the site, either in their entirety or as a teaser with a link that directs viewers to the institutional home page or online archive. NHF, for example, posted a fifty-six second low-quality video entitled "Fort Knox, Prospect, Maine 1936" in 2006. In early 2010, the video had been viewed on YouTube over 3,000 times, which is likely 300 percent more views than it would have received if NHF had not posted it on YouTube.

Context is extremely important to archivists, Snowden Becker, founder and board member of the Center for Home Movies, told me. It provides meaning to moving images, particularly when it is older material and the knowledge of it has been forgotten or lost. In addition, many archivists bemoan the fact that when users watch material on YouTube, it usually becomes "a YouTube video"; its presence on YouTube trumps its origins in or relationship to any other locus of cultural production. "There's a potentially pernicious flattening and equalization effect of having everything that moves available in one place. It makes establishing that all-important context, or the authoritativeness or authenticity or integrity of a piece of video, very difficult indeed," Becker said "and these are values that are pretty sacred to archivists."

The ubiquity of YouTube heightens archival anxiety about accessibility, but the low level visual quality of YouTube videos also creates unease within the archive. While low-resolution files are great for streaming, they corrupt the original image's clarity, grain, color, and the overall appearance of archival media. Archivists' thoughtful, thorough restorations attempt to recover the pristine nature of the original images, and some archival restorations (as will be discussed in chapter 5) may take decades to complete. When a ripped DVD version of restored film (and it happens all the time) appears on YouTube or when an archive posts its own material, the lovingly restored images can be visually degraded. In some ways, YouTube brings us back to days when older films were primarily viewed by way of cheap television programming, for YouTube corrupts the visual clarity of moving images, helping to give the popular impression that older films are inherently scratched, faded, out of focus, and simply hard on the eye. Clearly YouTube and other similar hosting sites highlight some of the present-day concerns surrounding technology, accessibility, and image modification that archives are not in the position to easily resolve.

The contemporary archiving community places high value on protecting artifactual authenticity and simultaneously strives toward comprehensive user access. The development of the American Film Institute (AFI) and the colorization controversy that led to the National Film Preservation Act (NFPA) both helped to shape the culture of the present-day film archive and its struggle to balance the principles of authenticity and access. The original purpose of the AFI was to put national dollars behind the training of the country's filmmakers so to heighten the quality of United States filmmaking. The archival movements initiated by the National Archives, the Library of Congress, and the Museum of Modern Art (MoMA), were, in part, guided by intellectual interests about cinema and United States history. The AFI's interest in film preservation and accessibility was motivated by a capitalist-nationalist ideal of producing good filmmakers. Guided by the New Frontier philosophy and the film industry's capital, the AFI dreamt of technological advances that would enable cheap image reproduction so that filmmakers would have easy access to the country's "best" films.

The AFI opened the ideological gates for accessibility during the second half of the twentieth century, ushering in a new archival era. One of the challenges that the AFI faced was how to replicate films efficiently and inexpensively in the 1960s and early 1970s, during an era right before the revolution in image reproduction. The technological dream of accessibility as well as the popular push for it became a reality a decade or so after the AFI became an institution; however, the innovative technologies that brought about the ability to replicate films inexpensively also created the capacity for people outside of the archival setting to alter the structure and meanings of canonical films.

Motivated by profit and enabled by technological advances, the colorization of classic films during the 1980s challenged the country's memories of Hollywood cinema by tampering with the original intentions of the nation's most well-loved filmmakers. Taken seriously by critics, the press, the public, and the government, the colorization threat revealed the ways that classic Hollywood films had become a part of the nation's popular memory and also had the potential to generate profit for those who owned the rights to them. Colorization also revealed a significant and troubling fact about the cinematic artifact: powerful people and new technologies could dramatically alter films sitting safely in the archive. The film archive could not guarantee a fixed and stable cinematic memoryscape.

It is important to briefly explain film copyright and fair use—thorny subjects that have routinely plagued the archival community. Because archival holdings often have complex copyright status, fair use is an ambiguous term that is difficult for people to interpret, and legitimate copyright owners are often reluctant to give permission to archives to allow access to their materials. Essentially, copyright law guarantees a copyright holder a series of exclusive rights for public performance, distribution, reproduction, public display, and the right to prepare derivative works. After the agreed upon period of time, the copyrighted work falls into public domain if the copyright is not renewed. Works in the public domain can be appropriated by anyone in any way that they wish to use them. As discussed in chapter 1, motion pictures were not covered by copyright at all until 1912 when the Townsend Amendment included them in the kinds of works that were covered by copyright. Prior to the 1976 Copyright Act, copyrighted works entered the public domain after twenty-eight years. In 1976, copyright was extended to the life of the author plus fifty years, and in 1998 the Copyright Term Extension Act added an additional twenty years of protection to works that had been published prior to 1978. Currently, fair use of copyrighted material is often the most complicated issue that users (and consequently archives) confront. Determining whether copyrighted material falls into fair use is guided by four rather ambiguous fair-use tests in section 107 of the Copyright Act: the purpose and character of the use, the nature of the copyrighted work, the amount and substantiality of the portion used in relation to the copyrighted work as a whole, and the effect of the use upon the potential market for or value of the copyrighted work. The potential for and fear of copyright infringement has shaped the culture of the film archive since its beginnings and continues to beleaguer the archiving community.

The American Film Institute Proposal

While the period during World War II helped to cultivate the first major attempt at creating a national film collection, it was, to a large extent, the effects of the Cold War and President John F. Kennedy's drive for excellence in the sciences that brought about the next profound national development in the film-archiving field. The national fixation on science and technology during the Cold War led to a perceived lack of national support for the arts and humanities. To correct this imbalance, Congress signed into law the National Foundation on the Arts and the Humanities Act on September 29, 1965 (its predecessor, the National Arts and Cultural Development Act of 1964 was also significant). The declared purpose specifically states that a civilization such as the United States "must not limit its efforts to science and technology alone but must give full value and support to the other great branches of man's scholarly and cultural activity." The act outlines broad frames of support for the United States to be a world leader in the arts stating that "the world leadership which has come to the United States cannot rest solely upon superior power, wealth, and technology, but must be solidly founded upon worldwide respect and admiration for the Nation's high qualities as a leader in the realm of ideas and spirit. Motion pictures, music, dance, drama, folk art, creative writing, architecture, painting, sculpture, photography, graphic and craft arts, industrial design, television, radio, tape and sound recording were some of the arts specifically named and defined as art within the law's text.

At the signing of the National Foundation on the Arts and the Humanities Act of 1965, President Lyndon B. Johnson emphasized the significance of film as a national priority. "We will create an American Film Institute, bringing together leading artists of the film industry, outstanding educators, and young men and women who wish to pursue this 20th century art form as their life's work." Congress, following Johnson's signing of the act, appropriated $2.9 million for the creation of the National Endowment for the Arts (NEA) and $5.9 million for the National Endowment for the Humanities (NEH). While the sums were modest, the signification was not; with the creation of the NEA and the NEH the U.S. government was overtly encouraging and supporting cultural and art activities with federal dollars for the purpose of promoting and extolling individualism, freedom, and pluralism, qualities that Communism wished to obliterate. It is not a coincidence that federal support for the NEA and NEH remained strong throughout the Cold War and began to diminish as soon as it came to an end. The United States' drive to promote the arts and science during the Cold War, in effect, led to the creation of the American Film Institute. While it was conceptually bundled with the NEH and NEA, the AFI had the strong private support of the financially powerful film industry, which provided the AFI more autonomy from the government than other art and cultural forms supported by the NEA and NEH.

Critics, scholars, filmmakers, archivists, and industry leaders had been considering and planning the creation of a national film institute a few years before Johnson signed the National Foundation on the Arts and the Humanities Act. Colin Young, the Los Angeles editor of *Film Quarterly,* in collaboration with Robert Hughes, the New York co-editor of the journal, detailed a proposal for an American Film Institute in the 1961 summer issue of *Film Quarterly.* It is an important proposal because it outlines an early plan for the AFI, but it also details the state of the American film archive in the beginning of the second half of the twentieth century.

Young explained that the impetus for the proposal came about during a 1960 Antioch College symposium about film exhibition. "It immediately became clear that considerable experiment in exhibition methods would be necessary," Colin explained, "if the meritorious films already lying neglected in vaults were ever to reach the audience for which they were intended."[1] The symposium participants concluded that traditional distribution and exhibition processes did not easily accommodate archival and contemporary art films. If innovative filmmakers had a difficult time showing their work, it could lead them to stop making films, Young warned. Echoing Iris Barry, he noted that the quality of film scholarship was unreliable because scholars did not have access to these films and had to rely upon memory or secondhand judgments. "This by now should all go without saying," he wrote, "but we find that we have to say it over and over again. We must preserve films and make them available for study."[2]

Only the MoMA's Film Library was capable of serving as an academic resource for film scholars in 1960. Young mentions the Eastman House's collection, but notes that it is a privately endowed institution that does not have a circulating program, and scholars who can afford to travel to

Rochester, New York, to view films in-house must also pay a fee. The Library of Congress and the National Archives, Young notes, has considerable archival holdings but provides few services because Congress offered little support. "Because of insufficient financing and shortage of personnel," Young wrote, summarizing the systemic problems, "curators have to make impossible decisions—to acquire or to preserve, to preserve this and not that, to buy new films or circulate the one they have, to acquire and preserve but not make available for study or reference and so on."[3] The film institute, Young proposed, would ameliorate some of these problems by encouraging, promoting, and assuming responsibility for educating the public about the value of film as an art. Young reasoned that if people were aware of the value of film it would be easier to find public support for film preservation.

Though film accessibility and availability was one of the primary reasons for developing a national film institute, the proposal does not focus upon an archival plan; in part, because of a planned Hollywood motion picture and television museum that would be responsible for building a strong collection of American cinema. The museum was intended to be a solution to the Hollywood tourist problem. "The studios' interest in the Museum has been sparked by the possibility it represents for solving one of their oldest problems in public relations—what to do with the millions of people who flock annually to Hollywood," Young writes, "and wish to see something being shot at a studio."[4] The plans for the museum, which was never built, sketched out a motion picture complex with one-way glass walls that would enable film production crews to do their work without distraction while throngs of tourists watched. Extremely ambitious in its comprehensive design, it included a museum, a film archive, a library and academic complex, theater, sound stage, television studio, and administrative office. The museum would also be the academic center for the movie industry.

While Young and his cohorts did not imagine a national archive, they did envision a need for a national catalog of films and film materials. "There is no central, reliable source of information about credits, titles, content etc., except in those cases where a film has been copyrighted through the Library of Congress," Young writes, "and even here the amount and type of information given varies."[5] The institute's cataloging role was imagined as a national catalog for film students and film users. Though the proposal provides few details for how to pay for and create a centralized motion picture catalog, one thing seemed certain: something needed to be done to improve existing conditions.

> At present this entire area of cataloging, and of making available catalog materials is so dispersed, that even veteran scholars are discouraged from the attempt to uncover it. Films should be of interest to the historian, the social scientist, the psychologist, and the economist, as well as to the aesthetician and the motion picture critic. But the difficulties rebuff most candidates, and kill the spirit of enquiry.[6]

The proposed institute would function to centralize services that would promote ways to educate the public about film. Young imagined the institute coordinating education efforts, making arrangements for short-term exposure to films of merit from around the world by way of a national film theater and a film festival, and helping to distribute undiscovered films. "None of this is any longer merely a dream," Young concludes, "It must and will happen. The outlines of responsibility are clear. The first steps are before us. It only remains to take them."[7] It is likely that the American Film Institute proposal would have been more complex if Young had known that the Hollywood film archive museum would never be constructed. The AFI proposal also suggested a series of centralized services that would benefit the film industry, filmmakers, critics, scholars, and film audiences; the plan's primary purpose was to increase public exposure to art, foreign, and unrecognized films. Young's proposal suggests that some films are more "art-like" than others and deserved the sort of exposure that the proposed American Film Institute could provide.

In September 1965, a month after the Hollywood museum site was paved over, President Johnson promoted the idea of a national film institute at the signing of the National Foundation on the Arts and the Humanities Act. By 1965, however, the purpose for the institute had changed. The new reason for establishing the American Film Institute was for fostering the talents of American filmmakers so to enhance the quality of film so no other country could rival the United States in production. Young's desire to facilitate the exhibition and distribution of the "unusual" or "undiscovered" film was no longer the central mission of the proposed AFI. The original spirit of intellectual inquiry had been put to rest.

The Stanford Research Institute White Paper

After the National Endowment for the Arts (NEA) was formed in 1965, the agency sponsored and financed a study for the purpose of developing plans for an American Film Institute (AFI). The Committee on Film, under the direction of writer, director, and producer George Stevens, Jr., the son of the acclaimed and prolific director George Stevens, retained the Stanford Research Institute to conduct a research study for assessing film education in the United States and abroad, the needs for archival services, the organizational possibilities of the AFI, location requirements, and financial possibilities and participation. Stevens, who would become the founding director of the AFI, was no stranger to the film industry. His pedigree, his own success in the film industry, his tenure as the head of the United States Information Agency's Motion Picture Division, and his interest in preserving his father's legacy made him a perfect fit for the AFI.

Stevens's role as head of the USIA Motion Picture Division was instrumental in pushing the government toward creating a film institute, and it also helped to situate Stevens as the AFI's first director. USIA-made films generally focused on U.S. policies and their positive relationship with other countries' agendas, counter-propaganda, and depictions of American life that helped to illuminate U.S. policy. Stevens was working on his father's films as an associate producer in 1961, when USIA director Edward Murrow asked him to contribute to the New Frontier by leading the Motion Picture Division.[8] While an analysis of the USIA film project and Stevens's successful direction of it is beyond the scope of this chapter, Stevens's ability to recruit talented filmmakers and oversee the production of interesting, well-made films had a powerful influence on President Johnson and his push to create a government-backed film institute that produced high-quality filmmakers (no doubt the 1964 USIA documentary about Johnson called *The President* was also a contributing factor).[9]

The Committee on Film published the findings of the Stanford Research Institute study entitled *Organization and Location of the American Film Institute* in February 1967. The development of the AFI was ultimately for the purpose of fostering the creativity and developing the talents of American filmmakers. Promoting excellence in filmmaking, the Stanford study explains, would enrich the quality of films in the United States and consequently would help to enhance audience's appreciation and enjoyment of films. "An American Film Institute, then," the study concluded, "can effectively improve film art by assisting in upgrading the discovery, education, training and opportunities afforded potential film makers."[10] The primary focus of the AFI would aim toward the professional training of filmmakers. The institute itself was imagined as a bridge between the academic and the professional realm of film; it was likened to a teaching hospital where theoretical and practical work is combined. The study states that while there were many sorts of film, the AFI would initially focus primarily on theatrical feature films and their creators because one of the organization's primary objectives was to promote film as an art form. Throughout the study, the Stanford authors consider the fiction film more than other kinds of film, privileging Hollywood, its primary benefactor again and again. "Although primarily a medium of artistic creation in the field of dramatics," the study explains, "film also is a historical and sociological record and a means of information storage for scientific, industrial and other purposes."[11] The study also claims that the most talented and successful filmmakers are "within the theatrical segment" of the film business.[12] In order to promote fictional film as an art and foster the education and talents of filmmakers, the study stressed the importance of an accessible comprehensive film collection for student filmmakers, film scholars, and educators.

Accessing the Moving Image

The Stanford Research Institute study underscored that student filmmakers needed to watch films in order to learn how to make them. And if film students needed to see films as part of their college and university training, then they needed access to a large film collection. The Stanford study and the development of the AFI were instrumental in opening the door to archival access, an issue which had always been complicated by private collectors and copyright laws. Historically, private film collectors had a tendency to ignore copyright laws believing that such laws were not relevant to their personal enjoyment of the films. Usually, private collectors, who amassed an enormous amount of films during the first half of the twentieth century, were able to maintain their collections without legal problems.

Film ownership grew much more complicated, however, when collectors opted to donate films to archives, sites that necessarily had to pay attention to copyright laws. "The interplay between archives and collectors goes back to the beginning of the movement and has had ebbs and flows. No one has wanted to discuss it too openly," Paul Spehr explained to me.[13]

Archives that had a heft of films from private collectors were naturally concerned that some of the holdings were infringing copyright laws. For this reason, some archives preferred to maintain a low level of access. It has been suggested that the George Eastman House historically maintained a low level of accessibility precisely because the archive was built by way of the 850 privately collected films of film preservationist James Card. The relationship between private collectors and archives shifted with the establishment of the AFI, Anthony Slide explains. David Shephard, the AFI acquisitions manager, and Lawrence Karr, AFI archivist, openly courted private film collectors with much success, though there were legal battles once some of the private collections became more visible.[14]

The authors of the Stanford study noted that the inability to access films for examination and study, more than any other factor, put film at a disadvantage over other arts in the United States. A national film institute could ameliorate this issue by offering a national storehouse of motion pictures, making film copies available for study, establishing cinematheques in major cities, offering cataloging and indexing services, sponsoring special film programming and exhibition, and subsidizing the study and publication of information about film. The study conceived of an organization that would privilege access so to improve the quality of filmmaking that would subsequently elevate the artistic level of the motion pictures in the United States.

The Stanford authors proposed that copies of original prints would be necessary to make moving images available to filmmakers and scholars. In the early twenty-first century, this idea hardly seems worth mentioning since the circulation of moving images is commonplace, and film scholars and filmmakers have access to a wide variety of films. Both old and contemporary motion pictures are available on cable television, videocassette, and in digital forms such as DVD. Copies of many motion pictures can be purchased or borrowed, and archival accessibility for researchers has increased tremendously in the last four decades. But in 1967, mass-market duplication and transfer and relatively inexpensive exhibitory innovations were not yet entirely conceivable.

The costs, time, and labor of duplicating the country's 35 mm films to make study prints for the AFI were staggering. The technical means exist, the study explained, so that a film copy could be accessible to "virtually anyone at anyplace." However, the study cautioned that duplicating the entire United States annual film output would cost $4.7 million (more than $26 million in 2010 dollars). Reflecting upon the most appropriate technological systems for viewing study copies, the researchers speculated that there was a possibility that some adaptation of the "in-flight projection system used on commercial airliners or the development of specialized 8 mm cartridge-type systems could be used to minimize special development costs."[15] More than a decade before the introduction of VHS and Beta to the mass market, the study concluded that it would be best for the AFI to modify film reproduction systems and components under development for other purposes so to increase the availability and accessibility of film.

The Stanford Research Institute study could only speculate how the country's film collection might be inexpensively copied and circulated to filmmakers and scholars. Yet their speculations about possible ways to do so pinpoints a historical moment when there was a national call for a broad circulation of films at a time when technological innovations for an economical duplication, transfer, and exhibition of films were not yet readily available.[16] Soon after the study's call for the democratization of moving images, movies would begin circulating much more broadly and fluidly. Older, independent, and international films, both well known and obscure, became part of the popular landscape during the 1970s and 1980s. The advent of cable television, the inexpensive video recorder and cassette, and the dramatic increase in film departments and programs at colleges and universities helped to ensure the infusion of motion pictures across the nation.

To be sure, plenty of moving images would remain ensconced in studios, archives, and private collections during the 1970s and 1980s. But at the beginning of the twenty-first century, the Stanford Research Institute's vision for the proliferation of moving images has been nearly realized. Of course, the dramatic increase in access to motion pictures was not a result of the Stanford study or the work of the AFI. Mass-market innovations and commercial distribution networks were the agents that eventually and rapidly broadened access to moving images.

Archival Coordination and Access

Issues surrounding the difficulty of accessing films led the Stanford authors to consider the conditions of the film archive in the United States and abroad, as well as the state of coordination and cooperation of the four leading U.S. film archives: the Library of Congress, the George Eastman House, the National Archives, and the Museum of Modern Art. According to the study, many important resources were housed at the four film archives, but the archives did not have enough information about one another's holdings and there were problematic gaps in each archive's collection. There was much work to be done to create a cohesive, comprehensive, and organized national collection. "The gaps in existing archival collections either have been or could be determined individually," the study explains, "but no overall assessment has been made either to consolidate knowledge about existing deficiencies or to develop objectives for the content and coverage of the archival holding that should be available in the United States."[17] That there was not institutional coordination toward a national film collection in 1967 is not a surprise. As shown in chapter 1, film collections and archives were not readily adapted and constructed in the United States. The moving image archives that did exist had only been active for a relatively short period of time.

The Stanford study includes a description of three outstanding foreign archives: the Gosfilmofond of Russia, British National Film Archives, and the Cinémathèque Française, as national examples of archives that house comprehensive national film collections. Besides highlighting the large collection and technical capability of the Gosfilmofond, the study notes its extensive cataloging capabilities. The British National Film Archives receives a nod for its extensive collection of films (many of them U.S. features) and its extensive exhibition and publications. Besides the 30,000 films it houses, the Cinémathèque Française was distinguished for its vigorous programming. The inclusion of these world-renowned archives in the study is significant when we remember the impetus for the study and the construction of the AFI: the American government and industry aimed to secure its reputation as the best filmmaking nation in the world. The moving image equivalent to the Sputnik crisis a decade before, the study focuses on the world's foremost archives to reveal the deficiencies of the moving image archival system in the United States. In order to lead the world in filmmaking, moving image collections needed to be comprehensive; an extensive cataloging system needed to be established, and the country's four leading archives needed to launch a more wide-ranging exhibition of their films.

The Stanford Research Institute study outlines the aims of a comprehensive archival system, but it also foresees the difficulties of accomplishing those aims. First, there are many historical works that cannot be recovered, and recovery will only get more difficult in the future because the deterioration of older films will continue to worsen. Second, funneling all of the United States' significant films and related documentation into a national archival system is a Sisyphus-like task because of the country's huge output of films. And third, the authors foresaw problems with the legal control of both private and corporate ownership of films held in archives. Nonetheless, the study authors imagined a foreseeable future when copyright laws might change for use of films for educational and noncommercial use.

The study does not suggest that the AFI would be the geographical center of access or that scholars and filmmakers would be granted access to archival projection prints at the AFI. Rather the authors suggested a number of locations across the country where prime archival materials would be made available. "In many cases," the study explained, "the proportion of total archival holdings required to be accessible at each location and the needs for any additional library locations can be determined on the basis of demand and the patterns of usage which develop in practice."[18] Proposing a handful of film centers in strategic geographic locations likely aimed to reduce the unspoken problem of moving image accessibility: east coast proximity. It was typically the geographically privileged—those who lived in New York or Washington, D.C.—or the institutionally privileged film scholars and filmmakers who had the easiest access to archival films. The Stanford authors were suggesting a geographic shift so to create new opportunities for archival access.

The study includes a map of the United States that plots the potential locations of the AFI. The headquarters of the film institute were proposed for Washington, D.C. (along with services such as education, exhibition, and research and planning). New York is on the map as a site for archives, a branch of information services, an industry liaison, and exhibition. But when looking at the map there is westward movement: the Midwest (a star is planted on Chicago but does not name it specifically) and Southern California are coordinates on the AFI map. The Los Angeles area is the proposed site for the Advanced Study Center, along with other services such as professional training, archives, and a branch of information services, exhibition, and an industry liaison. Southern California was the geographic pulse of the film industry; since the study had determined that access to moving images and education was an integral element to improving the country's filmmaking, at least part of the United States moving image archival culture needed to be transplanted to the West Coast.

The study concisely details the problems that lay ahead for the development and coordination of archival resources and the creation of a comprehensive national film collection. If the study had traced the United States' archival past, its readers might have been surprised by the swift development that had taken place since Iris Barry and her staff at the Film Library began collecting films. When the study was published three major institutions (MoMA, Eastman, and Library of Congress) held more than 23,000 principal films and the National Archives held some forty-seven million feet of film, from newsreels to captured enemy collections. So many films had been archived over a thirty-year period that the central issue had changed from a lack of archived films to the problem of coordinating the massive amount of films and film-related materials that had been collected.

Beyond the coordination of the country's film holdings, the study suggests that the nation needed better information about its films. It argued for an organized consolidated database that detailed the existence, availability, and sources of films produced in the United States. It proposed that the AFI might be the central clearinghouse that would facilitate the exchange of cinematic information. Such a centralized clearinghouse would help determine the critical gaps in collections and also improve scholarly film research by reducing the time and resources spent identifying and tracing films. The authors determined that scholars, filmmakers, and archivists needed specific and distinguishing information about films such as length, subject matter, content, audience level, key personnel, and technical characteristics in order to best understand the nation's motion pictures.

Similar in nature to the authors' consideration of the best procedures for copying films a decade before the mass marketing of the VCR, the study considered how to manage huge amounts of data about the nation's films. While computer technology, the authors imagined, would one day efficiently manage tremendous amounts of information, the costs remained prohibitive in 1967. The authors wrote that, "A high-capacity computer installation (IBM System 360, or equivalent) typically costs upwards of $1 million dollars, or an equivalent rental rate of $200,000 per month including related peripheral equipment. Development costs for new major computer program systems typically involve 15,060 man-years of effort and costs of from $500,000 to nearly $2 million."[19]

The Stanford study authors conclude that while the AFI needed to focus its attention upon accessibility and information storage and retrieval, it would need to adapt and modify advanced systems and components being developed for other purposes because of the exorbitant costs of development. The mass marketing of computers and software that began full force in the 1990s has enabled the film archive community to record, store, and make publicly available a tremendous amount of data about films somewhat efficiently and relatively inexpensively. Nonetheless, information accessibility is still one of the primary problems and aims of the archival field. Even with the great advances in technology and the drastic reduction of computer and software costs since the 1967 study, keeping track of the huge output of films, managing the relevant data, and making the information accessible is still a complex issue for the archival field, as we shall see in later chapters.

The American Film Institute and Moving Image Preservation

The findings of the Stanford Research Institute study and the creation of the American Film Institute in 1967 helped to construct a national platform for moving image preservation in the United States. In June 1967, the NEA awarded the AFI $1.3 million. The Ford Foundation also contributed $1.3 million, as did the Motion Picture Association of America. The AFI, headed by George Stevens, Jr., moved forward quickly developing a preservation mission that included generating public interest in film preservation, creating a cooperative agreement with the Library of Congress, as well as creating a formal relationship with other moving image archives (the Archives Advisory Committee). The American Film Institute Collection established at the Library of Congress enabled the AFI to acquire films while the library assumed the responsibility of storing and caring for them and making reference prints available to scholars and students. The AFI archivist Sam Kula explained that the institute's role was "to stimulate and coordinate a national film collection at the Library of Congress comparable to the national collections of cultural artifacts at the Smithsonian Institution."[20]

The AFI helped to shape the direction of moving image preservation in the United States for the remainder of the twentieth century.[21] According to Sarah Ziebell Mann, the AFI successfully publicized the crisis of film decomposition to Hollywood filmmakers and supported U.S. film archive preservation activities. However, the AFI filmmaking school in Beverly Hills, the Center for Advanced Film Studies, channeled funds away from the institute's archival activities. During the early 1970s, most of the institute's energy and financial support was focused on the filmmaking school. Unfortunately, once its start-up funds were gone, the AFI had difficulties finding new sources for funding its preservation activities.

Ten years after Colin Young's proposal was published, Ernest Callenbach, the editor of *Film Quarterly*, published an article entitled "The Unloved One: Crisis at the American Film Institute."[22] By 1971, the institute was in financial crisis and was widely criticized because of administrative issues, financing dilemmas, and personnel relations. His critique of the AFI focused mainly on its mission of educating filmmakers at the Center for Advanced Film Studies, and he viewed the resources that were thrown in the center as a waste. Callenbach suggested that the AFI needed to refocus its attention on developing film culture in the United States by concentrating on the archive, education, research, and distribution. Essentially, these were the very areas that Young had proposed the institute focus on ten years earlier. While much seemed to be wrong at the AFI, the archival and cataloging work had been, according to Callenbach, rather successful. The AFI has saved 5,000 films and established a catalog of American theatrical films offering researchers a centralized source of information. However, Callenbach suggested (if the AFI should make it through the crisis) a committee could just periodically assess the preservation work of the Library of Congress.

The AFI, in 1972, published *The American Film Heritage: Impressions from the American Film Institute.* In it, filmmakers, film scholars, critics, and archivists reflected on films and film techniques and technologies within the AFI collection (and maintained by the Library of Congress). In the introduction, Sam Kula, the AFI archivist and assistant director, detailed the preservation categories of the films included in the book: films lost and found by AFI efforts; films that had survived as a staple of late-night TV but were in poor condition before being recovered by AFI; and films in great need of restoration through archival efforts. Kula explained that through a network of private collectors and contacts in the International Federation of Film Archives, the AFI was able to find some films that had not been in any studio vault, museum, or archive.

The relationship between private collectors and archives shifted with the establishment of the AFI. Anthony Slide explains that AFI acquisitions manager David Shephard and AFI archivist Lawrence Karr openly courted private film collectors with much success, though there were quite a few legal battles once some of the private collections were publically visible. He also explained that some of the films had never disappeared from view but were in poor condition. In these cases, the AFI attempted to secure good quality 35 mm prints or preprint material so better quality prints could be made available for scholars and students. Finally Kula stated that some recovery efforts were even more dramatic. He wrote, "Three examples should indicate the complexity of the work: *The Power and the Glory,* in which an incomplete negative and sound track acquired from the studio was completed by material from Preston Sturges' own copy; *The Front Page,* where the film with a poor sound track was acquired from a foreign archive, and the sound track added from Vitaphone discs loaned by a private collector in San Francisco; *The Emperor Jones,* which was pieced together from several surviving 16 mm prints, a few feet, and sometimes a few frames at a time."[23]

Surely, these were rather sophisticated and refined categories of film preservation for many readers of the book in the early seventies. Interestingly, the rest of the book barely mentions preservation; most of the writers focus on the significance of the films, implying that without the AFI, these important films essentially would not exist—because they would not be in a national collection and available for study and exhibition. One of the book's messages is that the films the AFI saves not only help us to understand a chapter in art history, but they are also significant cultural artifacts. "What we are gradually learning at the same time is that the films also have significance as historical and sociological documents," actor Gregory Peck explained in the foreword. "They retain the power not only to delight us, but to enlighten us as well. As art and as history, they are being secured and preserved as a valuable part of our cultural heritage."[24]

While advocating that film preservation allowed for documenting the growth and maturity of the cinematic art form, Kula also suggested it is important to preserve films for their significance as historical artifacts. "The Institute's archivists recognize that because films reflect the social milieu in which they are produced, capture attitudes and opinions of the time, and record the changing nature of American society, they constitute a rich resource for students and scholars in many disciplines."[25] The mission of the AFI, of course, was to encourage and foster the talents of U.S. filmmakers; thus, it makes sense that AFI leaders reasoned that film preservation was most necessary for documenting the origins of cinema as art. But, Peck, Kula, and others of the AFI also believed that older films were like a time-travel machine, offering us a way to look back and see how life used to be. These two arguments for preservation existed simultaneously during the first half of the twentieth century as well.

In December 1974, Congress killed a bill that would have required the federal government to fund two-thirds of the annual budget of the AFI, changing the institute's capacity to be the focal point for national moving image preservation efforts. During the same period that the AFI was shifting its attention away from archival interests, the Film Archives Advisory Committee (FAAC) was developing as an organization composed of institutions focused on moving image preservation. "The archival organization FAAC was positioned as a collection of institutions," writes Mann, "all working toward similar preservation goals, but simultaneously craving independence from an overall national (and thus hierarchical) preservation structure."[26] The AFI's attempt to develop a national archival system was the United States' last try at such a singular, comprehensive plan. Slide explains that the AFI film preservation program cannot be dismissed. "A lot of good came from the AFI, particularly in the early years, but a lot of money and a lot of effort was certainly wasted," he writes, "in large part because of a lack of dedication from the higher levels of the Institute's administration."[27]

In 1980, Lawrence Karr, AFI administrator of the preservation program, reported in the *Quarterly Journal of the Library of Congress* that over fifteen thousand film titles had been added to the AFI collection at the Library of Congress by the end of 1979. The AFI continues to function as an educational institution for training filmmakers. And while it has been widely criticized for its inability to maintain a strong preservation agenda, it is important to remember that the AFI was developed for the purpose of fostering the talents of filmmakers. Preservation of and access to films was never more than a means to an end. Today the AFI helps to maintain the nation's cinematic heritage, principally by exhibition and the AFI Catalog of Feature Films.

The Stanford Research Institute authors' concern with coordination and cataloging was the first warning that managing the United States' archival films was going to be a complicated and taxing endeavor. Significantly, when Barry had begun to collect films for MoMA, one of her chief concerns was getting enough movies to constitute a collection. A decade later MacLeish and the members of the MoMA Film Library aimed to create a national collection of some substance and depth. By the time of the 1967 study, keeping track of the nation's film holdings was a problem that needed resolution. Today this remains a significant issue for the archival community. While there are technologies that have surely made cataloging and coordination much easier, there are also millions of more films, which have helped to create present-day cataloging chaos. The Stanford study cracked open the accessibility floodgates for the purpose of increasing and enhancing Hollywood's output, so to bolster the efforts of the Cold War. Situated at a point in history right before the explosion of technologies that enabled nearly anyone to control their viewing as well as significantly modify films at whim, the study's authors likely could not have imagined the complications that came with their dreams of accessibility. Intricately linked with commercialization, accessibility—such as the study proposed—required technological innovations that two decades later would unhinge the stable meanings of the archive that the AFI had attempted to institutionalize.

Colorization

For much of the twentieth century, those who advocated collecting, protecting, and restoring moving images reasoned that old films were evidentiary materials. Most adherents argued that saving old films was important because they were evidence of the origins of an important art. Others argued they were visual records of twentieth-century history. Generally, those who argued for the protection of films imagined a specific and particular audience for them. As we have seen, archivists and collectors argued that old films were for the edification of film scholars, historians, and sometimes sociologists and psychologists. Saving old films was important, curators and archivists argued, because they had the visual power to be significant scholarly artifacts. For much of the twentieth century, the rhetoric of film preservation characterized a search-and-rescue mission for future scholars. Near the midcentury mark, as cinema's reputation as an art form grew, the argument for saving and protecting films became more complex and intricate.

The protection and collection of films for the development and enhancement of filmmakers' growth as artists was an argument that emerged only after cinema had become an accepted art form, and film directors had been theoretically acknowledged as the primary artists of films. In the 1950s and early 1960s, film critics such as François Truffaut and Andrew Sarris reasoned that since film is a work of art, and since the artist shapes the art form, it is the director, more than anyone else, who shapes a film's distinctive quality. The idea of the "auteur" is often associated with the 1950s popular French journal *Cahiers du cinema*. It was the directors themselves—Truffaut, Jean-Luc Godard, and Eric Rohmer—who theorized the auteur. Innovators of this evaluative undertaking, they helped to generate an aesthetic of film that tended to privilege particular films and filmmakers over others. Often the preferred directors and films were from a different, earlier generation of filmmaking. "One of the most sweetly charming features of auteurism lay in its love for old pros or cinematic father-figures who were still alive," writes James Naremore, "making unpretentious genre movies or quiet meditative films such as John Ford's *The Sun Shines Bright*."[28] It is possible that the auteur theory and the older, sometimes forgotten films its theorists praised had an impact on the original argument for the creation of the AFI and the argument for the necessity of the archive in the Stanford study. If the future of American film required well-trained artists, then part of the training was to make sense of the best art that came before them—which required that they had the best of cinematic history available to them.

Film theorists did not dwell for too long on the auteur theory. Robert Ray explains that the events of 1968 helped to dismantle it. "The post-1968 period coincided with the development of academic film study, and although *auteurism* briefly persisted as a way of doing film criticism (aided by its explicit analogy to literary authorship)," Ray explains, "its apolitical concern with aesthetics suddenly seemed reactionary."[29] By the early seventies, psychoanalytic theory was influencing film studies, but mainstream culture maintained a steady focus on the film director. The filmmaker as both artist and celebrity became a normalized part of cinematic culture in the United States. And at no time in history was this more evident than when some of the nation's most popular filmmakers' work and the country's best-loved films—were altered. This meddling received nationwide attention and captured the popular imagination. The stability of the cinematic canon was also called into question when it became apparent that filmic images were easily altered by way of new technological innovations.

During the 1980s, filmmakers, Hollywood stars, and cultural critics of great prominence came together to argue for the protection of cinematic history. They also made a case for safeguarding the cinematic experiences for the viewing public—though this was not their principle argument. For the first time, the cultural significance of older films became mainstream news, but it was not a film scholar, filmmaker, producer, or archivist who managed to bring the country's cultural heritage to the nation's attention. It was a technique called colorization, a new computer technology that added color to black-and-white films. And while colorization does not have a specific or a rational relationship with the film archive or film preservation, it is important to this study because it led to a cultural sea change, as it brought visible attention to the nation's cinematic past, and it invited both the public and the national government to consider the significance of the country's film history and what it meant to safeguard it.

In 1986, critics began to loudly complain about the intentions of Ted Turner (who had recently bought the Metro-Goldwyn-Mayer film library), the Hal Roach Company, and Color Systems Technology because they began producing videocassettes of black-and-white movies with color added to them. The colorization process was first used to add color to the footage of the Apollo moon mission (as if people on the moon was not spectacular enough) in 1970. The end result of the colorization process results in a videotape of a movie with computerized color added to it. The inventor Wilson Markle founded Colorization Inc. and developed a process whereby technicians, with the help of a computer, determine the gray level of every object in each shot of the film and note movements of objects with shots. The computer then adds color to each object, while keeping gray levels the same as in the monochrome original. "Which color to use for which object is determined through common sense (green for grass, blue for the ocean) or by investigation," Gary Burns explains. "For example, movie studio photographs or costume vaults may provide guidance as to what color a hat should be."[30]

Film critics such as Vincent Canby and Michael Dempsey instructed the public in film history, aesthetics, production, and the ills of colorization by explaining that black-and-white films should not be understood as films that lacked color. "Black-and-white films are not color films accidentally made without color. Black-and-white films are lit and framed according to their own special needs," Canby explained in the *New York Times,* "if only, at times, to create a sense of depth that's more easily suggested by color."[31] Michael Dempsey expressed a similar idea in *Film Quarterly.* "Color may have been too costly for most American studio movies during the 1930s and 1940s, but once black-and-white photography was chosen," he explained, "the movies were designed, costumed, and lit accordingly."[32] Colorization, the critics complained, ruined moving pictures by adding inauthentic tints to films that required no color for their effect. "Colorizing is done by computers programmed to make white faces pink, gray trees green, black cigars brown," writes Richard Mooney, "These hues bear little resemblance to a movie made in color, though; they are like a black-and-white postcard that's been watercolored over."[33]

Those who supported colorization during the 1980s, namely film producers and others who could financially benefit from it, argued that colorization had no impact whatsoever on the original film because the colorization process adds color to a video transfer and does not alter the film print. "Colorization isn't about film. It's video," Ronald Haver, curator of film at the Los Angeles County Museum explained. "Our cultural heritage is safe in the archivists' vaults. This is Turner's stuff, and he can do what he wants with it."[34] Haver explained no archivists had come out publicly against colorization because the process necessitated archival attention to films undergoing the process. Pristine prints of a black-and-white nitrate film had to be made before being colorized. While colorization ensured the preservation process, it still threatened to disrupt public memory.

Another argument for colorization was that new audiences would get exposure to old films as a result of their premier broadcasts on cable television and release on videotape. And because colorization required new prints, the film quality would be a vast improvement over what viewers had been used to seeing on television. "Yes, I'd certainly prefer to see a screening of 'The Music Box' from an original black-and-white 35-milimeter print, along with hundreds of other Laurel and Hardy fans at some theater," one viewer opined. "But that's rarely possible or convenient, and I'll take that color version I saw on Thanksgiving Day, any day over the previously available, horrid version I'd seen on TV before."[35] This particular viewer's argument represents the view of the informed and discerning spectator who can differentiate between films produced in color and colorized films. The knowledgeable and active consumer who enjoyed the novelty of colorization and found entertainment in watching colorized prints but also recognized that colorization was not the part of the original intention was rarely a consideration in the very public debate.

The most powerful argument against colorization came from Hollywood filmmakers and stars, sometimes the very people who had made or starred in the films being colorized. The aesthetic quandaries of colorization were part of their argument against the process. In 1986, after watching seven minutes of a colorized version of his film *The Maltese Falcon* (1941), John Huston said, "It would almost seem as though a conspiracy exists to degrade our national character. It's as though our children have been sold into white slavery and now the Turner organization has dyed their hair."[36] In 1987, in a videotaped message (to a congressional hearing on the legal issues raised by adding color to films), Huston asked, "Why should this mindless insipidity be allowed? Why should Humphrey Bogart and Mary Astor, who were so careful about their images, be bushwhacked by the coloroids?" Before the same panel Ginger Rogers lamented: "All those lovely girls in *42nd Street* suddenly had the same orange face, the same orange legs, the same green costume and the same blank look." Rogers read a statement from James Stewart who bemoaned the colorization of Frank Capra's *It's a Wonderful Life.* "Gloria Graham played a character named Violet, so someone thought it would be cute to have all her costumes in violet. That is the kind of obvious visual pun that Frank Capra never would have considered." While Woody Allen (who also participated in the hearing) had other issues with colorization he also disliked the visual effects of the process. "Right now it's like elevator music. It has no soul," Allen wrote in the *New York Times.* "All faces are rendered with the same deadening pleasance."[37]

U.S. laws generally privilege the property rights of copyright holders. In the case of moving pictures, this means that filmmakers have few rights over their creations because copyright holders are usually film studios, production companies, or wealthy individuals like Ted Turner who can buy film studio libraries. While critics, filmmakers, and stars alike disliked the aesthetic effects of colorization, their campaign against the process hinged mostly on the fear that the few rights directors had were further eroded with the colorization of films. While most critics cringed at the aesthetics of colorization, they argued for legislation against it based on their belief that it violated the rights of a filmmaker. Allen, who became a spokesman for filmmakers and critics against the colorization process, explained that those who wished to colorize films had disdain for both artists and the film audience. "I believe the people who are coloring movies have contempt for the audience by claiming, in effect, that viewers are too stupid and too insensitive to appreciate black and white photography—that they must be given, like infants or monkeys, bright colors to keep them amused," Allen said. "They have contempt for the artist, caring little for the moral rights these directors have over their own creations. And finally they have contempt for society because they help define it as one that chooses to milk every last dollar out of its artists' work, even if it means mutilating the work and humiliating the culture's creative talent."[38]

Of course, from the earliest days of film exhibition, films have been cut and altered by exhibitors in a variety of ways, making them shorter or eliminating scenes considered objectionable. Once films began being broadcast on television, the original integrity of films were further compromised because techniques such as pan-and-scan were used routinely, and films were cut and chopped up for the sake of commercials. While colorization is essentially no different because it does not affect the film in its original form, it was the tipping point. It is not clear why it was this particular filmic manipulation that so entirely offended filmmakers, stars, and critics. Allen explained that it was "the preposterousness of colorization" that was "the straw that broke the camel's back." "Where will it go from there?" Milos Forman asked. "Why not jazz up a little the music in *Gone with the Wind*? Kids are today heavily into heavy metal, so let's replace the soundtrack with electric guitars and drums."[39]

Paul Grainge argues that colorization angered so many, because it was a "flagrantly commercial venture with no artistic pretensions; it was bankrolled by a media magnate for whom property rights were paramount."[40] But the anticolorization faction did not base their arguments on property rights, the rights of the film spectator, or the integrity of the cinematic artifact. Rather their rhetoric focused on the aesthetic infractions upon films that were considered part of the country's cinematic canon. "By digitally reinterpreting a monochrome movie," Grainge explains, "colorization was seen by its detractors to compromise not only a film's authenticity, but also its place within cinematic history."[41] There was also a fear that over time black-and-white videotape copies would disappear, leaving only colorized copies readily available to consumers. Those financially invested in the colorized process, it was argued, would not see fit to make new videotape copies of the films in black and white; thus, the colorized videotapes could eventually push the original black-and-white version into oblivion.

For our purposes, it is important to put the controversy of colorization in historical context. Its significance is, in part, the somewhat unintended effect of ushering in a new era: the more organized and centralized effort of protecting the country's cinematic past. We must also consider what the colorization controversy can tell us about cinema, history, and evidence in a particular historic moment, the moment prior to the nation becoming immersed in digitization. As we have seen, during the second half of the twentieth century, the filmmaker obtained a privileged position in the United States. The Stanford Research Institute study and the American Film Institute reflected this change. As the seventies and eighties progressed, cinema studies departments grew and multiplied, and while a new generation of film theorists resisted canonical formations by way of postmodernism, film scholars, students, filmmakers, and archivists still worked to construct a cadre of older films and filmmakers that they considered culturally significant.

A canon is an abstraction but it is also a process whereby leaders in a particular field determine what particular works of art, what specific artistic pleasures generations of people should share. It is an idea that, in theory, binds people together. The imagined corruption of that canon, I believe, was the impetus for the politicized nature of the colorization controversy. The computerized coloring of films such as *The Maltese Falcon, It's a Wonderful Life,* and *42nd Street* was troubling because those films were part of the film canon that a generation of filmmakers, critics, and film students and fans had helped to construct. Even though colorization did not tamper with the films themselves, the process interfered with the memories of the original films, as well as how those against colorization imagined the films would be remembered in the future. In the case of colorized cinematic classics, it was not the archival artifact or the historic evidence that mattered. The corrupted circulating copy was the cause of panic. Filmmakers and critics believed that the process would alter the cinematic memoryscape: while colorization brought classic films back into wide circulation, made them widely accessible, it also distorted and interfered with the memories of them.

The irony of the colorization conflict is that while it ultimately helped to promulgate and advance the protection of the United States' cinematic heritage by way of the National Film Preservation Act, it also highlighted the belief that the film archive could not maintain, protect, or help to construct a singular cinematic meaning for any film, including classical Hollywood films. The process of colorization revealed that filmic meaning was not necessarily tied to or correlated with the cinematic artifact protected in the archival vault. Because the circulation of film depends upon its mechanical and electronic reproduction, its worth does not and cannot lie in singularization. Thus, cinematic value is not dependent upon the singular filmic artifact. With a slight of the hand, colorization altered the agreed upon meanings and intentions of classic and well-loved films, and all the while the filmic artifact remained untouched in the archive. The colorization controversy revealed the tenuous link between the cinematic artifact and its cultural meanings; it exposed the fragility of the tie that binds the film archive and cultural memory. The colorization case suggests a questionable and frail connection between cinematic artifacts and their imagined future meanings and uses.

The Director's Guild of America hoped to influence Congress to institute new legislation protecting films from any technological changes that could infringe upon the filmmakers' original intentions, but such legislation was never realized. In 1988, Representative Robert Mrazek, a Democrat from New York, and Sidney Yates, an Illinois Democrat, introduced legislation for the creation of the National Film Preservation Board (NFPB). The purpose of the thirteen-member panel was for selecting twenty-five films per year that were deserving of protection against any alteration not authorized by their makers. If technological processes, such as colorization, ever altered the films selected by the NFPB, a disclaimer would have to appear at the beginning and end of the film when it was broadcast on television. There were many objections to the bill. Filmmakers like Woody Allen welcomed the idea that legislators were attempting to deal with the issue of filmmakers' rights, but saw the bill as only the first step. "Unless this is the first crack in the armor that leads to a law protecting the rights of all artists to prevent changes of any type whatsoever to their work without their consent," Allen proclaimed, "then I would say it's meaningless."[42]

It seemed that film producers, those directly involved in the colorization process, and television broadcast executives did not object to the disclosure statement on films approved by the proposed board, though they had some objections to the proposed bill. "It is desperately wrong for the Government to get into the motion picture business," Jack Valenti, the president of the Motion Picture Association of America, stated.[43] Though he favored full disclosure of any alterations to films, Valenti believed that a voluntary process, like the ratings system, would be better. While the Turner Entertainment Company already labeled their colorized films, Roger Mayer, the president of the company pronounced, "Taste and choice should not be legislated."[44]

On September 25, 1988, President Ronald Reagan signed the National Film Preservation Act into law, which read:

> Directs the Librarian of Congress to establish a National Film Registry to register films that are culturally, historically or aesthetically significant. Prohibits any person from knowingly distributing or exhibiting to the public a film that has been materially altered, or a

> black and white film that has been colorized and is included in the Registry, unless such films are labeled disclosing specified information. Sets forth specified exceptions.

The National Film Preservation Act, according to Slide, is a misnomer, as the act had nothing to do with film preservation. "It is all rather ridiculous," Slide explains, "an exercise in bureaucratic futility, designed primarily to confuse the American public into believing that Congress has, in some mysterious way, arranged for certain important American film to be preserved."[45] Tom McGreevey and Joanne Yeck believe that the NFPA directly confronted the issues raised by film colorization. "The act did address these concerns, at least as far as the Registry list was concerned. Films included on it were to be preserved in their original form *and*, if they were released on video in an altered way, were to be labeled as altered."[46] Grainge declares it a conciliatory political gesture that put the "legal primacy on property while, at the same time, it validated the *principle* of artistic inheritance."[47] The National Film Preservation Act was undoubtedly a misnomer, but it was also a rather uncomplicated idea, which provided momentum for a shift in the country's view of its national cinematic heritage. The NFPA lifted the nation's cinematic history into the light, and it marked the beginning of the contemporary scene of the film archive in the United States, which is the subject of the chapters to follow.

It is worth noting that while the National Film Preservation Act of 1988 was significant for helping to instigate a cultural sea change, the demise of colorization as both a practice and a controversy was not a result of the act. Following the passing of the bill, labs continued to make colorized films, which continued to be broadcast on television and sold as videotape cassettes. The colorization practice dwindled and died primarily because of economics. The novelty of colorization diminished and colorized films stopped being interesting to the viewing public. When colorizing films stopped being a profitable endeavor, they stopped being made. Philosopher Julie Van Camp argues that the fascination of the colorization process diminished as a result of the infiltration of the culture of computerization during the 1990s. "In this environment we are no longer shocked or dazzled or startled by the capabilities of technology," Van Camp explains. "Colorization seems a downright trivial, almost ancient technology with issues somewhat clear and unambiguous, even if we do not all agree on the desired outcome."[48]

Conclusion

During the 1987 colorization controversy, the sociologist Bernard Beck argued for protecting the rights of artists but also warned readers of the dangers of stifling creativity spawned by technological innovation:

> If the current movement against colorization can produce relief for that indignity and lead to institutional and societal protections for the arts, the quality of life in America will be greatly improved. But the creation of official academies must not be an occasion for suppressing the rise of vigorous new creative forms. The monolithic marketplace will not be much impaired by the creation of some sacred exemptions for works of art. New technologies will soon bring unimaginable creative possibilities into the hands of brash young artists and ordinary people who enjoy playing. Our reverence for past artistic achievements must not obscure our appreciation for new directions, even when it means tolerating the irreverence of those who follow them.[49]

Beck's sagacious commentary reflects the dialectic tension that the contemporary archival community routinely faces: how to be the caretaker of authenticity in a consumer culture seemingly hell-bent on upending it. In the years before the establishment of the AFI, accessibility was rarely touted as an archival virtue, but once accessibility became institutionalized, archivists were encouraged to open their doors to the public by way of the technologies that threaten to debase the authenticity of the artifact (and its cultural memory) that they aim to protect. The archive is not yet able to compete, and the general public is yet to be convinced that there is any more pleasure in the archive than there is in the YouTube environment and that sanctioned archival images are any more interesting than the thousands of modified films that appear on YouTube each day.

Grainge argues that the fight to protect canonical cinema has the same conservative impulse as the fight to keep multicultural literature and history out of the curriculum. "Both engaged rhetoric of opposition based upon the stability of tradition," Grainge explains, "the need to maintain aesthetic value, the preservation of authenticity against fakery, the impositions of the marketplace, and the continuities of cultural and historical transmission."[50] Grainge links the colorization controversy with the conservative and nostalgic impulses of the period, but the nation's canonical anxieties would have an even greater influence on film preservation and the archival community in the early 1990s, when the media-savvy Christian Right walloped the NEA with criticism for supporting controversial art and artists. As a result of the Right's successful battle against moderate Bush Republicans and the NEA, the NEA lost power, prestige, and money, and as an indirect consequence, the funding of the AFI was greatly reduced. Film preservation's financial hit caused alarm in the archiving community, and in 1993, the battle to protect the nation's filmic heritage took center stage once again, this time in the form of two congressional hearings.

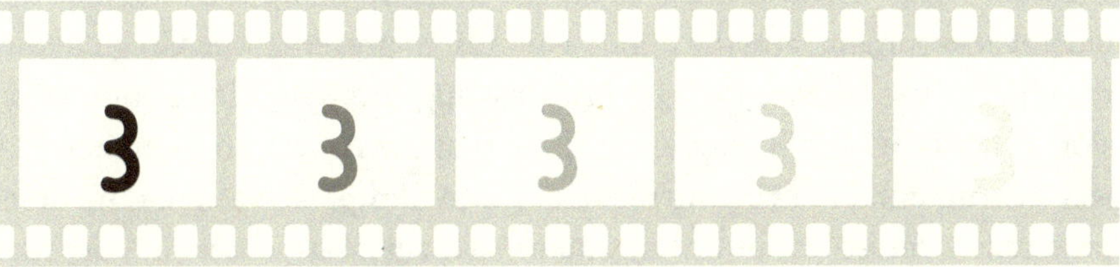

FILM PRESERVATION 1993

Orphans and the Culture Wars

The colorization controversy inadvertently brought film preservation into the national spotlight, but it gained national attention in other ways as well. Martin Scorsese, film preservation's most famous spokesperson, began fostering awareness and generating financial support for film preservation more than two decades ago. In 1990, Woody Allen, Robert Altman, Francis Ford Coppola, Clint Eastwood, Stanley Kubrick, George Lucas, Sydney Pollack, Robert Redford, Steven Spielberg, and Scorsese created the Film Foundation, an organization dedicated to preservation and the protection of filmmakers' rights. Through fundraising and monetary support, the Film Foundation supports preservation and restoration at the Academy Film Archive, George Eastman House, the Library of Congress, MoMA Film Library, UCLA Film and Television Archive, the National Center for Film and Video Preservation at the American Film Institute, and the National Film Preservation Foundation. The Film Foundation has supported the preservation of five hundred films since its inception in 1990. Scorsese, more recently, was instrumental in the founding of the World Cinema Foundation in 2007, a nonprofit organization that has similar preservation goals but with an international focus.

The twenty-four-hour classic movie network, American Movie Classics, which began on-air film preservation festivals and fund-raising in 1993, had an explicit preservation agenda and brought national attention to the nation's cinematic legacy. While DVD technology did not arrive on the national scene until 1996, VHS technology and cable channels heightened access to and awareness of classic films, spurring the industry, the federal government, and the public's interest in preservation. Greg Lukow, the chief of the Motion Picture, Broadcasting and Recorded Sound Division at the Library of Congress told me that the American Film Institute was instrumental in bringing recognition to film preservation. One of its primary successes was promoting national archival awareness in ways that individual archives were never able to do alone.

Lukow also explained that archival expansion led to a greater awareness of old films; from the late seventies to the early nineties new archives were regularly appearing on the regional and national scene. "One or two new archives were opening a year," Lukow told me. "It really snowballed in the early nineties with the establishment of AMIA (Association of Moving Image Archivists). It was a major step in the establishment of archiving as a profession." The United States began producing more moving image archivists and preservationists in the last two decades of the twentieth century than ever before, and as the profession grew, the voices of the archive gained national attention and recognition. In the 1990s, the United States Congress began working closely with the Librarian of Congress, James Billington, to create a platform for national conversations about the film archive and preservation, leading to widespread and organized preservation efforts, as well as concise documentation of the voices of the contemporary archive.

As part of the National Film Preservation Act of 1992, a study was completed on the state of film preservation in the United States. The National Film Preservation Act of 1992 mandated the four-volume *Film Preservation 1993: A Study of the Current State of American Film Preservation*. The co-authors Annette Melville and Scott Simmon researched and co-wrote the Librarian of Congress report, in consultation with the National Film Preservation Board. Melville is currently the director of the National Film Preservation Foundation and Simmon, her co-author, is a professor of English at the University of California, Davis. Simmon and Melville conducted research for seven months, interviewing as well as gathering information through library research, public testimony, and written statements from more than one hundred organizations. Volume one is a preface and interpretation of the public testimony. Volumes two and three are transcripts of the two National Film Preservation Board public hearings held in Los Angeles on February 12, 1993, and in Washington, D.C., on February 26, 1993. Volume four is a collection of written statements from people unable to attend the hearings, as well as additional comments from the people who participated at the hearings. The report "lays the framework for a planning document," write Melville and Simmons, "which will present to Congress a national strategy for coordinating film preservation, developed in consultation with archivists, copyright holders, educators and others concerned with the survival and accessibility of American film."[1]

The study and the plan promoted film as an art and a vital link to the cultural memory of the twentieth century; it advocated for an increased public awareness of the need to preserve motion pictures and also helped to shift the federal government's preservation funding focus from Hollywood cinema to orphan films. These goals, with the exception of a new priority on nonindustry films, echoed those laid out by the MoMA Film Library, the Library of Congress, the National Archives, and the AFI during earlier decades of the twentieth century. The report is a snapshot of film archiving and preservation as it was practiced and understood in the early 1990s, revealing predominant themes and ideological stances that eventually came to influence the shape and character of archival culture in the early twenty-first century. The report describes the current "moving image archive crisis," defined as the disappearance of moving image history caused by a lack of concerted effort to preserve the filmic past. The report also shifts the definition of the cinematic canon, calling for a casting of a wider net over the types of films that needed preservation. The report advocates for the preservation of amateur, regional, experimental, and industrial cinema, and films made by and about minorities.

By the early 1990s, film preservation was an accepted and integral method for protecting the cultural memory of the United States. That film is critical to the construction of twentieth-century cultural memory is a privileged assumption throughout the four volumes of the study, for without intervention by way of film preservation, the twentieth-century historical record would be greatly compromised. Much of the film preservation discourse around the 1993 hearings was an appeal for a more inclusive and diverse cinematic record during a period of federal funding setbacks for preservation.

The Problem

When film preservation gained national attention as a result of the colorization conflict, it was powerful Hollywood directors and actors who brought it to national attention and ultimately led Congress to pass the National Film Preservation Act of 1992. When the Librarian of Congress issued the film preservation study, the new advocates for old films were not only members of the film industry but were also archivists, film preservationists, and scholars. Corruption by way of colorization was no longer the chief concern; rather, in near unison, the archiving community voiced concern that if more films were not preserved appropriately, the history of the twentieth century would be compromised.

The first sentence of the Executive Report summary asks, "What are we doing to save America's film heritage for future generations?"[2] Several assumptions work together to construct the preservation crisis in the Executive Summary. The first belief is that film preservation is critical to the twentieth-century historical record. The second assumption is that it is the federal government's responsibility to preserve its cinematic heritage. The Executive Report acknowledges that both past and current film preservation efforts have been, overall, an abysmal failure: "there is universal agreement that more must be done in the few remaining years of this century if the next generation is not to look back on current efforts as little more than a tragic failure."[3]

The Culture Wars and the Film Preservation Crisis

The impressive list of preservationists, scholars, and other experts who gathered at the congressional hearings had well-articulated arguments for film preservation's calamitous state. One of the arguments that both the Executive Report and the spokespeople at the hearings make clear is that preservation requires a great deal of money and federal funding had recently been greatly reduced. "While public interest in saving older films seems never to have been higher," the Executive Report explains, "federal funding continues to decline and is now less than half of what it was in

1980."[4] One of the reasons for the decline in federal funding was that the National Endowment for the Arts (NEA), the organization that helped to fund the AFI, experienced some serious setbacks in the early 1990s. For twenty some years, NEA has been funding the AFI, but that funding was compromised when the NEA received a body blow during the culture wars. "The funding troubles of the NEA," Greg Lukow explained to me, "is not a factor to be overlooked in this transition. At the same time, Congress became interested in film preservation during the late eighties."

The NEA became a casualty of the culture wars during the late 1980s and 1990s when the Christian Right—Pat Buchanan, Jesse Helms, Pat Robertson, and Lynne Cheney and others—zeroed in on the NEA's "moral failings" as a wedge issue between the Christian Right and moderate Republicans. "The Bush administration had one cardinal goal for the arts: keep them quiet," writes Richard Jensen. "It failed because a resurgent Christian Right discovered enough cultural sins in the NEA to energize its ranks, and political commentator Patrick Buchanan realized this was a wedge that would prove to true conservatives they should dump Bush."[5] Their biggest targets were the museum exhibitions of Robert Mapplethorpe's homoerotic photographs, Andres Serrano's Christ-in-urine photograph, Karen Finley's performance art, and a PBS television program about homosexuality. The media savvy Christian Right pointed to these exhibitions and programming and defined them as cultural ills that the NEA supported with tax dollars. Their campaign against the NEA was successful and Congress responded to the heat by amending the law that created the National Endowment for the Arts to bar the use of NEA funds to promote arts that were obscene, homoerotic, or depicted sexual activity.

By the beginning of the nineties, Congress eliminated some of the new restrictions on the NEA, but by then it had lost some of its financial power and national reputation. President Richard Nixon's NEA had a $131.6 million budget; during Jimmy Carter's administration, the NEA had an all-time high budget at $255.7 million. President George H. W. Bush's NEA had a budget of $177.1 million, and by the time Bill Clinton became president in 1992, the NEA budget was reduced to $167.5 million.[6] After Congress constrained the NEA, it funneled its reduced budget to major museums rather than individual artists, in part so that museums could conduct the rigorous vetting process of artists. The NEA budget cuts also reduced AFI film preservation funding. This helped to bring about the early

1990s film preservation crisis, which led to the congressional hearings, the publication of the Executive Report, and ultimately the creation of a film preservation plan that privileged pluralistic and culturally dynamic orphan films.

Building the Case for a Shift in Funding Priorities

Paul Spehr, the assistant chief of the Library of Congress's Motion Picture, Broadcasting and Recorded Sound Division explained in his testimony, during the congressional hearing, that the resources that helped to fund film preservation at the library dried up during the 1980s. During that same period, the costs associated with preservation increased substantially. Besides the practical problems with funding, Spehr also suggests that preservation costs more in 1993 because the preservation efforts in the 1990s were more sophisticated.

> So now we are now having to look at the contents of a number of cans, maybe getting on the phone and calling up the Museum of Modern Art or George Eastman House, or working out an exchange arrangement to exchange material from institution to institution, borrow material from commercial sources. We spend a good deal more time creating the kind of work that we should have been doing from the beginning. The results are much better, but our ability to produce it has been declining at a rapid rate because there has not been an increase in resources.[7]

Robert Rosen, the director of the UCLA Film and Television Archive echoes Spehr, dramatizing the vast problem confronting the archives. "I think most of the archivists around the country would say that well-meaning statements of concern are not enough, consciousness raising is not enough, any number of bake sales and charitable activities like that are not enough," Rosen argued. "There must be a bottom line of the report, in order to satisfy the needs of archivists across the country confronting the deterioration of film in their vaults."[8]

Mary Lea Bandy, the chief curator of film and media at the Museum of Modern Art, explained that during the fifteen years prior to her testimony, the museum had to raise $500,000 from foundations to make quality materials, replace prints, and increase access. "It is ironic," argues Bandy, "that as public awareness of the importance of preservation has broadened, it is very, very difficult to raise money today to support our film projects. Government and corporate funding is shrinking, partly because everyone continues to ask the same questions: 'Shouldn't the film studios fund the archives? Aren't the film studios realizing a profit from the release of our films on video?'"[9]

While declining preservation financing, the fragility of film material, the battle with time, and human neglect are all constructed as enemies of film, during the congressional hearings the film industry is one of film preservation's most oppressive opponents. From an archival perspective it was not difficult, during the hearings, to construct the studios as adversarial. Film studios, for example, held the copyrights to the films they deposited at the Library of Congress. As a result, the library became the studio films' custodian. They are cataloged, stored, and in some cases, preserved—with little help from the studios. However, the copyright owners are frequently reluctant to give permission to public access to the films that are cared for in and by the public interest. The Librarian of Congress, during the Washington, D.C., hearings, passionately detailed and summarized the problem:

> We have people who own copyrights who do not want even a single viewing by a scholar in a lonely booth. There is, moreover, no clear acknowledgment of responsibility and very little concrete help from the owners, so in general the taxpayer is doing this at the moment and the industry is not. . . . Are they serious about their own heritage or not? Or do they just want to throw receptions and parties, talking about it but not doing anything about it, while the people who are doing something about it are being kept alive by the public.[10]

While the Librarian of Congress expressed the way many preservationists viewed the contributions of the private studios at the hearing, the studio spokespeople, who were also invited to the hearings, articulated their positions as well. Most of them explained that they were doing significant amounts of preservation work on their own materials but admitted they had not contributed to the larger preservation effort or community. Gray Ainsworth from MGM explained, "I think that, yes, the feeling—I believe the national feeling of responsibility and pride to preserve moving images and cinema—is definitely there. I just don't think the specifics have been defined well enough."[11] Chairwoman Fay Kanin asked studio representatives if their companies might be willing to allocate funds to film preservation beyond their own holdings—to contribute in a way that went beyond their own company's needs. Their responses highlight how they perceived their responsibility to a national plan of preservation. "Paramount is spending an incredible amount of money doing this already," Philip Murphy stated, "I'm not sure how we could justify anything beyond what we're already doing." "We cooperate with UCLA Archives from time to time on various Republic projects contributing money and material," Ernest Kirkpatrick explained, "I don't think this idea would fly." "I would say it's a possibility with us," Ainsworth from MGM said. "Obviously I can't commit to anything but we—you know it sounds like a good idea, but also a very touchy one."

Judging from the studio representatives' remarks, they were concerned about film preservation, but were focused upon their own studio libraries—most likely so the studios could generate revenue for the still relatively new home video market. Historically, of course, studios were unconcerned with most of their older films, and the public archive stepped in to rescue them. It is not difficult to understand why those associated with the public archives might have felt some rancor toward Hollywood studios. Throughout much of the twentieth century the studios were the primary beneficiaries of the archival agreement even after they started taking care of their own collections. By 1993, as the Executive Report argues, it was the rare studio that failed to protect its library. Nonetheless, the report also explains that the studios have a long way to go: "True, preservation information on individual titles is not publicly available, and studios still have a significant number of unprotected titles (Sony Pictures, for instance, estimates that it still must convert to safety film about 50% of its 840 Columbia nitrate titles)."[12] By the early 1990s, studios such as Sony, Universal, and Disney were doing some cooperative projects with public archives, as well as funding some staff positions at the Library of Congress in order to provide service to studio-deposited and donated nitrate films. The studios were integral to the formation of the problem; their hesitancy and reluctance to provide real support for a national plan for film preservation provided archivists, scholars, and even the Librarian of Congress a space for the archival community to rhetorically push new preservation and financial responsibilities on to the studios, so that what was left of federal funding could focus on orphan and non-Hollywood films—films that often come with less copyright problems and are often less costly to preserve than Hollywood feature films.

The Orphans Are Rescued at the Hearings

As we have seen, Hollywood film has been at the center of most archival efforts during much of the twentieth century, and it certainly was a major focus at the Los Angeles hearing. Many archivists today would argue that early preservation efforts did not save enough Hollywood films, as well as suggest that many of the early preservation efforts should be done again. However, at the 1993 hearings, archivists, scholars, and studio representatives explained that there were other kinds of films that also needed attention. Many archivists argued for the consideration and preservation of newsreels, home movies, industry films, documentaries, avant-garde, and independent films. This is a dramatic departure from the way film preservation had been imagined and carried out in the past.

This new way of thinking about films is historically significant because it changed the cultural value of non-Hollywood film, furthered the discursive crisis (for now there were many more films that would require preservation attention), and most important, helped to construct a new priority for the national government's funding for preservation. The "orphan" film made its national debut on the film preservation stage and was secured as part of the archival lexicon during both congressional hearings. An orphan film, generally speaking, does not have an apparent copyright holder and lacks commercial viability; thus, it does not have much of a chance of any persons or institutions paying for its care or preservation. The introduction of the term at the congressional hearings has been attributed to David Francis, the then chief of the Motion Picture, Broadcasting and Recorded Sound Division at the Library of Congress; however, Philip Murphy at Paramount Pictures was likely the first speaker at the hearings who used the term when he said, "There is a great need for the Library of Congress and Congress to focus on the parts of American visual heritage which do not naturally fall under someone's ownership. We speak here of that great collection of public domain material much of it on nitrate film. Those titles are called orphans because they have no protectors, no organization with the wherewithal to transfer the material to safety film to assure that future generations will have the opportunity to view what the early part of our century looked like on film."[13]

At the end of the twentieth century, the cultural importance of cinema and the need to preserve it was not a new idea, but the championing of the smaller, lesser-known, alternative representations of the twentieth century was. "Traditional preservation efforts directed largely toward the Hollywood feature seems shortsighted," the Executive Report states, "in light of the relative neglect of other types: newsreels, documentaries, experimental or avant-garde films, anthropological and regional films, advertising and corporate shorts, dance documentation, and even amateur home movies, especially of ethnic groups invisible in mainstream media."[14] This list suggests a staggering amount of films that would require preservation, but it also conjures a different way of considering what is cinematically important.

Many of the archivists at the hearings spoke to preserve orphans and non-Hollywood films. The archivists, curators, filmmakers, and scholars who advocated the preservation of these kinds of films were interviewed for the study, invited to speak at the hearings, and were asked to provide written statements. Their participation suggests that by the early 1990s, a sea change was already occurring at the national level; the voices advocating for orphan and non-Hollywood film were recognized as important for the development of a new national plan, but with the reduction of federal funding for film preservation, the tremendous increase in the kinds and numbers of films that needed consideration put a greater strain upon how national resources might be allocated.

Those who spoke about orphan and noncommercial films must have been aware of the importance of their testimonies; they had an opportunity, in a national forum, to articulate why such moving images were culturally significant and a critical part of the country's cinematic heritage. But they also had to argue for their archival attention and funding. In his testimony, UCLA's Film and Television Archive director, Robert Rosen, stated that film of the twentieth century was important because of its entertainment value, but he argued that in order to justify saving moving images to the public and Congress, the benefits of film preservation must pertain to a variety of academics, critics, filmmakers, social planners, and policymakers. "Consequently, any plan for a national preservation effort must recognize this pluralism as a point of departure and must focus on means to assist the entire array of participants," Rosen explained. "In a real sense, the plan must be for all of us."

Rosen's commentary envisions preserved films as important documents for various types of investigation—stretching far beyond classic and Hollywood film. His argument necessarily escalates preservation's problem because "a plan for all of us" requires that many sorts of moving images must be preserved. Rosen points to the nearly invisible and unknown newsreels and documentaries in the UCLA archive as an example of the kinds of moving images that require governmental support: "At UCLA we have 25 million feet of invaluable newsreel material owned by the people of California." Equating the newsreels with cultural heritage he states, "this is a public trust."[15]

Karen Ishizuka, curator at the Japanese American National Museum in Los Angeles, was the first speaker at the Los Angeles hearing to articulate why noncommercial film was historically relevant. Ishizuka, the curator of a collection of 8 mm and 16 mm amateur film taken by Japanese immigrants and their American-born children, argued that such films were "never-before-seen visions of America." She explained that most historic mainstream moving images—including newsreels, documentaries, and fictional films—mostly offered mainstream white perspectives and portrayals. Ethnic groups' perspectives were absent and their portrayals were usually either stereotypic or blatantly racist. Thus, the home movies of Japanese immigrants and Japanese-Americans offered a significant contribution to filling this representational void.

Ishizuka recounted a poignant story told to her by one of the museum's film donors. A second generation Japanese American who began taking home movies in 1935, he was incarcerated in an American internment camp after the bombing of Pearl Harbor. He smuggled his movie camera into the camp, with help from a Caucasian foreman. While he could not shoot images of guards, barbed-wire fences, or watchtowers, he was able to capture daily life in the camp. In a letter to Ishizuka, he wrote, "I hope when you see—when you look at the scenes of Mochitsuki pipe repairing, dining hall duty and church service, you look at the spirit of the people. You will see a people trying to reconstruct a community despite overwhelming obstacles. That, I feel, is the essence of these home movies."[16]

When describing some rare interior moving images of a Japanese American bank, Ishizuka asserts that these images are not just vacations and birthdays; unlike commonplace domestic images, she explains, the home movies of civic and economic life were historic footage worthy of study and preservation. She reiterates that there are distinctions to be made. Not all home movies should be preserved: "Selectivity," Ishizuka explains, "as with all film considered for preservation, is key." To make this distinction at the hearing was rhetorically necessary. Even if Ishizuka imagined that all home movies were equally important, it would not have been wise to say so. The general anxiety about the cuts in funding for preservation hung in the air—and Ishizuka was the first archivist, in a national public forum, to argue for the cultural significance of home movies.

During the Washington, D.C., hearing Frederick Wiseman and Rick Prelinger made the case for why lesser-known, noncommercial films—specifically documentaries and orphan films—should be preserved. Wiseman, who at the time of the hearings had made twenty-six documentary films in twenty-six years, explained why documentaries should be part of the national preservation effort. He argues that documentaries will offer historians of the twentieth century a clear picture of the texture of everyday life—a sort of time traveling. Documentary films show how people talk, walk, dress, relate to each other, the nature of work, the social organization of society, family relations, the handling of deviant behavior, the operation of courts, the role of police, medical practices, the relationship between men and women, racial issues, the functioning of government agencies, scientific experimentation, the nature of entertainment and our music and the ways it was performed. Arguing that documentary film will be the future historian's primary window to the past, Wiseman suggests documentaries provide in-depth and transparent portrayals of ordinary life.

Wiseman argues for a national archival effort that collects and preserves such material, explaining that the current focus on Hollywood film inhibits rather than widens the historian's view. While documentaries can offer the scholar the quality and appearance of the mundane, Hollywood cinema offers a commercial glossy interpretation of popular culture. Comparing narrative Hollywood films to the best-selling novels of the nineteenth century, Wiseman said, "What interests twentieth-century historians of the nineteenth-century American life," Wiseman continued, "are not just the best-selling popular novels of the period, but documents that give the texture and feel of everyday life."[17] While Wiseman acknowledges that documentaries have political perspectives and particular points of view, he also asserts that the documentary is a form of "natural" history, as the documentary form lends itself to an enlarged and textured but transparent window to the past. This naturalized view seems to conjure an ultra materiality of the ordinary, lending itself to a kind of time travel that enables us to witness the immediacy of places located in history as well as the social interactions in the home, the street, and in the organization and institution.

During the testimony, Billington affirmed the value of the documentary asserting that viewers readily engaged with the documentary material on the Library of Congress's American Memory site. This easy engagement, he suggested, seemed to come from viewing the particular and the functional elements of everyday life. He suggests that such observations about the details of the commonplace stimulate inquiry and lead the public back to the library to find answers. "So this kind of experience forces people back into books, rather than pulling them away," Billington stated, "the way so much television does these days."[18]

Prelinger explained the power of film's immediacy and its mundane and profound nature.

> I have never seen people talk back, call out and interact with a movie like that audience did. . . . They saw the rich public life of Main Street crowded with shoppers, gawkers, and flirting teens, community rituals like proms, distributions of Christmas presents, and Memorial Day parades and the faces of people, their manners and body language of fifty years ago. One person even saw her older sister for the first time for her sister had died before she was born.[19]

At the time of his testimony, Prelinger had supplied industrial, advertising, and educational film footage to more than two thousand producers, researchers, and scholars. Having often witnessed noncommercial film's impact on audiences, Prelinger, perhaps more than anyone else, was able to articulate how these seemingly unassuming images fit into the cultural milieu. An archivist, writer, and filmmaker, Prelinger is a popular figure, one could even say, a celebrity in archiving culture. An articulate, unassuming visionary, Prelinger owned a stock footage company for twenty years that ultimately consisted of fifty-one thousand advertising, educational, industrial, and amateur films. Eight years after the congressional hearings, Prelinger donated his films to the Library of Congress, partnered with the

Internet Archive, and made two thousand of the films from the Prelinger Archive available online for free viewing, downloading, and reuse.

Prelinger's conviction is, in part, focused on nurturing the historical consciousness of future generations. Like Wiseman, he imagined a time in the future when people's understanding of the past would be shaped by vivid and moving records of the mundane and the ordinary. Rejecting the prospect of a future where access to the past and the construction of history is based upon images of life as interpreted by Hollywood, Prelinger shapes the way future generations envision the past by providing them with histories of the ordinary. "Their preservation and ready accessibility will send a powerful message to future generations," he stated, "that the history of daily life is not just a matter of nostalgia and quaintness but a means of understanding the heritage of our communities, lives and labors."[20]

Prelinger, like Rosen, convincingly argues that moving image preservation is an endeavor worthy of the nation's effort because of its populist agenda. "Somewhere in the forgotten industrial, advertising or educational film there is something for every one of us," he explained during his testimony, "scenes of our hometown, pictures of how our fathers and mothers worked for a living, a treatise on social etiquette or maybe the look of a twenties farm or fifties supermarket and you will not see many of these everyday images in newsreels and feature films."[21] These kinds of films are vivid and recognizable signposts of history for the ordinary time traveler. Creating a place for the mundane alongside the extraordinary, Prelinger helped to shift the way scholars and hoi polloi think about mundane cinema.

Many of the archivists and film preservationists during the 1993 hearings argued for a broader, more inclusive view of what counts and what matters for the future. The new archivists and curators opened the doors wide, making fewer distinctions about the artistry and canonical significance of particular sorts of moving images. Custodians of the future, they are grounded in the belief that almost all film matters, for it is impossible to know what future investigators will want to see and know. The new archivists are speculators rather than sages. A few speakers argued that there are some films that should be entirely ignored. But others like Jonas Mekas, the avant-garde filmmaker and artistic director of Anthology Film Archives cast a larger cinematic net and mindset. Mekas suggested that future generations of students and scholars will not only expect records of commercial films, they will also seek out records of daily life filmed by amateurs and documentary makers. His view of the human potential of home movies and documentaries is Romantic and transcendent. "They will see the human spirit move into more subtle aesthetic and spiritual spheres and they will be uplifted and transported into those spheres themselves," Mekas explained, "as we all are by the works of the great poets of the past."[22] He suggests that the future viewer will be spiritually uplifted. Moving images, ones created by non-Hollywood interests, can inspire the spiritual and artistic self. While amateur filmmakers have routinely championed the home movie, it held a lowly position in the cinematic hierarchy during most of the twentieth century. The claims for its transcendent power, at the hearings, helped to move the home movie up a notch or two in historical value.

Archival Access for the Taxpayers and Scholars

During the first wave of film archiving there was far less concern about access than there was during the early years of the second wave. There was substantial discussion, during the hearings, about the necessity of public and scholarly access to the collected, preserved/restored, and stored images. Some speakers, like film scholar Robert Kolker, an English professor at the University of Maryland, argued that access is essential to the preservation process. "To say that a particular title has been saved from deterioration, that a color, nitrate positive has been transferred to three safety black-and-white negatives and put in cold storage is a triumph indeed but an incomplete one," Kolker said. "What is the value of an expensive act of preservation if the results are inaccessible? If scholars and students cannot see the results, if the only access to the particular film is still through a scratched and spliced 16 mm dupe, or more likely, a poorly resolved video recording who profits from the preservation? Pedagogy and the history of film do not. The unseen remains the unknown."[23]

Kolker dismisses "the jewel in the vault" model of cultural preservation, but believes that students and scholars need to behold the best cinematic artifact available. The teaching of film and the construction of its history depend upon a clear and available view of the filmic object; neither an inferior duplication nor a restored beauty unavailable for public viewing can entirely enhance the cultural understanding of film. For Kolker, watching a film by way of distorted images (many times or not) cannot help to bring clarity to cinematic history. "At the very least," Kolker stated at the hearing, "I would suggest the Library of Congress should be enabled to make viewing copies of every film that becomes part of the preservation process."[24]

Mary Lea Bandy emphasized the importance of public access to the Museum of Modern Art's mission. She estimated that the museum showed somewhere between three to five thousand films a year. Preserved by the museum as well as other archives, these films are made accessible for scholars, students, and the public by way of their circulating library, rental to schools, private viewings, and the museum's public program. Like Kolker, Bandy believes in ideal ways of viewing archival cinema. She explained that she did not seek the rights to distribute the films on videotape. "We have a philosophical quarrel with that," Bandy explained. "We believe that we should be providing films for educational use as film."[25] But Bandy also acknowledged that conversion and distribution of videotape were problematic in terms of legalities and resources. Still, first and foremost, she places highest value on the publicly accessible cinematic artifact in its original form. "We have the right and the inclination to go to 35 mm in our 16 mm collection. And where we can, we are doing that on a very, very limited basis," Bandy said. "The videos that we distribute are videos of independent video art which the video artist has made. Or, in the case of the documentaries, we have made a major exception. For documentary programs made for television, if the filmmaker with whom we have the royalty arrangement, if the filmmaker distributes the work in both video and film, we will do the same."[26]

To know the history of film is to see it on film and as close to the original as possible. This is not a surprising philosophical stance for Bandy to have. She works at a museum where the exhibition of original forms is valued and expected. The final phase of the preservation process, in the film department at the Museum of Modern Art, is an exhibition print. Bandy defined an exhibition print as a film that the museum restores and also maintains its preservation materials. The exhibition print, a restoration that is as nearly complete as possible, can be circulated because the museum maintains its filmic elements. When the museum holds those parts of the film that are essential to the essence of the original film and when the film department preservation staff have completed its preservation/restoration, then the print can be shipped to various venues for exhibition.

Bandy explained that the print "could go all over the world and be shown everywhere because we have all the other materials." The global circulation of a museum-restored exhibition print, for Bandy, is an ideal example of accessibility. She aims for films to be viewed by a collective in a space of exhibition. The ideal preservation comes as close as possible to the original filmic form and original cultural context. Rubbing up against many original elements helps to construct an authentic history of the film, its context, and the cinematic past.

Two of the country's leading cinema scholars also attested to the desire to view and exhibit the most complete film, closest to its original form and format for pragmatic, pedagogical, and theoretical reasons. At the Washington, D.C., hearing, David Francis asked Douglas Gomery and Tom Gunning to detail the ideal materials for exhibition in the academic environment. During the hearings, Gunning reasoned that while there is a hierarchical scale, cheaper technologies such as video, videodisc, and laserdisc have important functions in the learning environment. But the ideal form for research is 35 mm: "I also, as an archive rat, have an extreme importance on [sic] the use of 35 mm for research and 16 mm for exhibiting to class rooms. But I think all of them have roles and I think they are all different."[27] In agreement with Gunning, Gomery specifically outlined why and when the original form is the best choice for constructing/understanding the history of cinema. Using widescreen cinema as an example, he explains that for students to understand widescreen cinema they need to see and experience it.

But aside from more practical considerations like viewing films in their original formats, Gomery also asserts that films need to be seen in their entirety. A media economist, prolific writer on the mass media, and professor of journalism at the University of Maryland, Gomery compared cinema to classic literature. Gomery explained, "I think it is just like a literary work, just like the complete version of Shakespeare or a complete version of *War and Peace*. I think it is part of the educational responsibility to expose people during their university training to the complete work, not some abridged or partly affordable work."[28]

To know a film and to create knowledge about a film, Gomery and Gunning assert, the scholar and student must be able to see it in its original and near complete form. Both film scholars acknowledge that viewing films in nonoriginal formats, using technologies such as videotape and laserdisc is beneficial, but scholars and students should view films in their most authentic form and format when they first encounter a film. "I think that the other technologies of videotape and increasingly laserdisc, because again of their affordability, can be used in subsequent screenings," Gomery stated. "Although, of course, if you are going to write a paper trying to argue the complexity of wide screen imagery in Douglas Sirk or Orson Welles or whomever, it is going to be pretty difficult unless you have access to original materials over and over again so you can make that kind of an argument and analysis."[29] Initial encounters and experiences with a preserved film should ideally be in its original form, but alternative technologies and formats are likely necessary. Historic analysis requires the most authentic format and the likelihood of a secondary technology so that the scholar can view a film in its original conception, as well as come to make sense of its significance by multiple viewings. While the ideal cinematic experience seems to be one that is as close to the original as possible; secondary formats and technologies suffice for prolonged cinematic study.

Other speakers at the hearings suggested that the public's access to preserved materials was entirely deficient. Brian O'Doherty, the director of Media Arts at the National Endowment for the Arts questioned the faith that the public should have in film preservation: "Who profits from preservation? Studios locating lost originals legally or illegally held? Specialized exhibitors? Home videos of tasty morsels? The usual ranks of admirable scholars? Well, where is the public?"[30] John Belton, a Rutgers English professor and member of the National Film Preservation Board (he published his important book *Widescreen Cinema* in 1992) wondered aloud how to define the public. Belton asked, "Specifically, is the public the academic community? No. The press? No."[31] O'Doherty said the public is the people in movie theaters and those who watch television, and while they pay for film preservation with their tax dollars—over a twenty-year period the NEA gave $10 million to fund nitrate preservation—they receive little in return.

Tracing the preservation cycle of a film such as *Cleopatra,* O'Doherty suggests that once a film is preserved it lies in stasis, and preservation without exhibition is a disaster. "It is preserved as if in aspic. For whom? That is the question that strikes terror into the heart of conservative preservationists, and it is a question that must be answered," proclaimed O'Doherty. "I have heard it asked several times today. For no matter how bright the radiant screen of their memory, the public will not long support preservation without seeing its results. The archives' costive habit does not invite a rush of educated patrons and donors."[32] Like many of the speakers at the hearings, O'Doherty reiterated that public monies for preservation were diminishing. The continuance and generation of new revenues would require a deeper and broader public awareness of what the preservation community actually does. O'Doherty said that if there were to be more money for preservation, the archival community needed to work harder to make their work visible, so to raise the public's consciousness.

Copyright issues also emerged at the hearings as a plague that inhibited the progress of film preservation and accessibility. Copyright holders—motion picture studios—do not always allow for public exhibition of the films that archives restore and preserve. During the hearings, movie studios took a hard rap for their lack of cooperation in the preservation process. Billington never specifically referred to motion picture studios as the unyielding copyright holders, but did rail against "special interest groups." He spoke passionately against copyright holders who deny public access to their films:

> I do not like to put it so bluntly, but I serve no interest except that of the Library of Congress, which is a kind of a cover name for the collective memory of the creative activity of the United States. And I find it very difficult to understand how we will be able to get higher visibility before the public for a national plan, unless those who have benefited commercially from this public preservation are more forthcoming. . . . But I find that every time we try to get further services of any kind out for the public; we are combated by the active opposition of special interest groups that are not doing these services, but somehow for some reason do not want to support, or want to actively oppose, the public's doing it.[33]

Other speakers worried that the public's generosity would diminish if the preservation community did not make their efforts more visible to the public. Some speakers worried about the public's attention span and potentially faltering desire to fund preservation, a process that takes a long time and is quite costly. The primary hindrance is the resistance of the "lesser publics" (as Billington refers to them). "Are they serious about their own heritage or not?" Billington wondered aloud at the hearing. "Or do they just want to throw receptions and parties, talking about it but not doing anything about it, while the people who are doing something about it are being kept alive by the public?"[34] The "rights problem" (as O'Doherty calls it) is formidable because the archival community (which he explains is "the world that represents our memory") and the world of commerce are vastly different from one another and have few avenues of communication. "At least they sit down and talk in the Middle East peace talks," lamented O'Doherty.

While all speakers did not express this frustration it is important to note that two powerful people from the "world that represents our memory"—the Librarian of Congress and the director of media arts for the National Endowment for the Arts—publicly articulated their dissatisfaction with studios' use of and resistance to the archival culture and its community. During the era of the hearings, studios and archives were not as collaborative as they were at the end of the twentieth century, and it stymied archival progress and thwarted public attention to restoration and preservation work. The archiving community put its collective foot down at the congressional hearings. With tightened preservation budgets, the voices representing the archive demanded that the studios begin to take more responsibility for preserving their own films, which would enable the federal government to focus its funding on orphans.

Television's Critical Role in Film Preservation

Throughout the hearings, speakers asserted that more public awareness of film preservation needed to be cultivated. During the early 1990s, there was no better model of public awareness than the American Movie Classics (AMC) television channel. Television and cinema have not always had an easy relationship; in the 1970s well-known directors, critics, and stars railed against the computerized colorization of classic Hollywood films broadcast on television. When the fear of colorization and its potential for canonic corruption passed, an easier relationship between Hollywood film and television broadcasting began. In the early 1980s, American Movie Classics was launched: a twenty-four-hour movie network dedicated to classic Hollywood cinema from the 1930s to 1970s.

The president of AMC, Josh Sapan, spoke at the hearings and explained the station's philosophy and its relationship with archival culture. The last speaker of the film preservation hearings, Sapan spoke eloquently about the relationship between cinematic art, national identity, and conservation. He highlighted the ways in which AMC worked with the country's archives and promoted their work. AMC seemed to be the model for the national promotion of classic Hollywood and a contemporary archival culture. While Ted Turner's conception of the relationship between television and cinema was the bane of those who revered the golden age of Hollywood, AMC seemed its redeemer.

Sapan claimed that film preservation and restoration were critical to the success of AMC, for its aim was to broadcast movies on television as "they were meant to be seen." The channel was actively involved in educating the public about this forty-year span of classic cinema. Sapan explained that AMC was committed to creating "a museum like environment on the television channel." Hollywood movies broadcast on a television seem to have little in common with a museum environment; however, the channel's aims were not that different from a contemporary museum mission. Sapan subscribes to a fundamental relationship between the objet d'art and the public, explaining that the channel is "providing the best experience we can for the viewers." AMC developed a relationship between classic cinema and its television audience through its devotion to original work in its most complete and original form. "In April 1990, I hope these details are relevant and not boring," Sapan said, "we presented the world premiere of the color-restored *Hell's Angels,* the classic 1930 Howard Hughes film featuring an original scene that is the only existing natural color footage of Jean Harlow."[35]

The best experience for the AMC audience, it seems, is the broadcasting of a cinematic artifact in which most or all of its original elements have been recovered and restored. Like the film department at the Museum of Modern Art, the AMC channel places the highest value on original cinematic materials and formats; however, it is impossible to ignore the fact that these restored, original filmic artifacts are broadcast on television. The original exhibitionary space for cinema is, by the logic of the television broadcast, impossible to recover, but this does not seem to be included in AMC's calculus of cinematic reception. While explaining why more national awareness and financial support for film preservation from the private sector was necessary, Sapan likened the disappearance and negligence of the nation's cinema to the destruction of a country's art during wartime. "In example after example, from Aleutian carvings to the spirituals of the slaves on southern plantations, from Russian art to Jewish humor, the culture and customs of a people really define them and help keep them alive," explained Sapan. "And while obviously we do not equate the destruction of books or films with the loss of human lives, the elimination or destruction of a society's or a culture's art is a rare and pretty terrible form of humiliation."[36]

For Sapan, the disappearance of film is a cultural humiliation. Without a cinematic record, a country is not entirely able to construct, maintain, and reconstruct its identity. The channel's mission and its philosophical approach to cinema exemplify the potential for the popularization of film preservation at the end of the twentieth century. While AMC helped to elevate old Hollywood cinema's status as an art form, it also helped to create an audience for it. By promoting cinematic restoration and preservation, AMC helps to elevate the popular status of archives and their collections.

The Storehouse of Twentieth-Century Culture

Scholars, archivists, and the Librarian of Congress were resolute in their belief that moving images are critical to cultural memory. Gomery, Gunning, and Kolker argue that film preservation is important so students and scholars can study, analyze, and then translate cinema's meanings and histories. The cinematic artifact requires careful study and such careful study will yield the truths of motion pictures, which will contribute to our knowledge about art, history, culture, and national identity. Prelinger, Wiseman, and Ishizuka believe historic moving images require little or no translation, nurturing historical consciousness by way of their immediate and experiential nature; viewers can understand the spirits of history without a translator. Both theories of reception, translation, and direct experience, are important to the hearings' preservation discourse, for by the early 1990s, cinema's place in the cultural milieu comfortably resided in both the museum and the town hall. At the end of the twentieth century, the archive had become the agreed upon storehouse of cultural memory, and it needed to contain a full range of films—from Hollywood classics to home movies—so to keep the past alive.

That all American citizens might shape their historical consciousness by accessing a wide array of cinematic genres necessarily changed the archival landscape; in the early twenty first century a colossal amount of film are in queue to be preserved, stored, and made accessible. Today archivists wrestle with managing and keeping track of the massive amounts of moving image documentation that have poured into archives since the 1990s. The present-day reality of archival surplus has dramatically changed the way archivists navigate and conceptualize their work, as we will see in the next chapter.

Preserving the Pluralistic Film Record

The National Film Preservation Foundation started its operations in 1997, four years after the congressional hearings and publication of the Executive Summary. Greg Lukow explained to me that the funding transition from the NEA to the NFPF greatly reduced federal support for preserving studio films.

> For years UCLA or George Eastman house or MoMA would submit through AFI-NEA film preservation. Now you can't do that. As the result of the National Film plan, the NFPF was established to allow the federal government to support orphan films only. It changed the way archives applied for grants and made collaboration with the private sector imperative because archives no longer get federal dollars for those kinds of films. It used to be UCLA, GEH, MoMA would get 70,000 or more annually from the NEA in grants. The NFPF seldom gives a grant for more than 10,000 dollars, but they give a lot more grants than the NEA because orphan film is a lower cost item in the industry.

With the NFPF focus on orphan preservation, film studios have given more of their attention and money to preserving industry films. "If you look at the archives that do Hollywood movies—LOC, UCLA, MoMA, the Academy, and the Eastman House—all of us combined couldn't preserve Hollywood history," Eddie Richmond, the former director of the UCLA Film and Television Archive told me. "We can help; we can do a lot. But if studio films are going to be preserved, it has to be in cooperation with the non-profit archives and the studios. In the last 20 years, some studios have created in-house departments and in many cases collaborate with the archives. It is a huge step forward."

Since the 1993 congressional hearings, it has become common practice for studios to underwrite some or all of the preservation work done by public archives with the Film Foundation serving as the facilitator between public archive and studios. The preservation process often works more efficiently in the archive than in the studio because archives can more easily secure the loan of film material from other archives, and studios generally have fewer trained staff to do hands-on preservation. Archives give studios access to preservation prints in return for underwriting the preservation. Studios make new masters and hope to profit from theatrical and DVD releases of the preserved and restored films. Well-known studio preservationists/restorationists Schawn Belston (vice president of Library and Technical Services at Fox Home Entertainment), Grover Crisp (vice president of Asset Management and Film Restoration at Sony), and Barry Allen (executive director of Broadcast Services and Film Preservation) regularly collaborate with archivists who work in public archives.

When the federal government shifted its attention to the preservation and restoration of orphan films, the national film record grew broader, more dynamic, and diverse. As of September 2009, the NFPF has financially supported the preservation of 1,563 films in forty-eight states, the District of Columbia, and Puerto Rico. To characterize the film list is difficult because the films are so wide-ranging, but the For the Love of Film: The Film Preservation Blogathon, which featured "Saved through the NFPF" films, offers a glimpse into the twentieth-century record that the NFPF is helping to preserve. The 2010 blogathon featured NFPF preserved films including the Ford Motor Company antiunion cartoon *Uncle Sam and the Bolsheviki—I.I.W. Rat* (1919); the Yiddish language musical spoof *Cantor on Trial* (1931); the African American contralto Marian Anderson's concert *Marian Anderson: The Lincoln Memorial Concert* (1939); the African American independent *The Blood of Jesus* (1941); *Trail to Better Dairying* (1946), a profile of a Maine dairy club; *The Magic Key* (1950), a U.S. Chamber of Commerce short about the powers of advertising; the documentary, *People of the Tundra* (1956), about Native Alaskan troops during World War II; *Alaska Earthquake* (1964), amateur footage of the most powerful recorded earthquake in North America history; *To the Fair!* (1964), a promotional short for the World's Fair; Sid Laverents's trick film *Multiple Sidosis* (1970); a Clemson University documentary about peach production *Peaches: Fresh for You* (1973); and George Kuchar's Hollywood-style staged screen test *I, An Actress* (1977). A small sampling of NFPF films, but this list suggests that the National Film Preservation Foundation is not only preserving a diversity of film styles, subjects, intents, and filmmakers' visions, it is also helping to build an inclusive and more sweeping record of the twentieth century that includes but does not privilege industry films and the dreams of Hollywood.

I helped to write a successful NFPF preservation grant for Tad Nichols's 1939 film *Navajo Rug Weaving*. Nichols is an important twentieth-century photographer of the Southwest and his artful eleven-minute amateur film documenting Navajo domesticity vividly depicts the weaving process. An important alternative to Hollywood stereotypical representations of Native Americans during the same period, the preservation of *Navajo Rug Weaving* ensures that weavers, Navajos, amateur film scholars, and historians of the Southwest will be able to access this filmic record of Navajo life outside of Flagstaff, Arizona.

It is the politics of the Christian Right that is partly responsible for the NFPF preservation of *Navajo Rug Weaving*, for in the struggle to define and defend canonical works, the Right helped to reorient the national film preservation agenda. The conservative Right, struggling against multiculturalism, the politics of difference, and postmodernism, fought to protect their singular national vision of art, literature, and history. Successfully reducing NEA and AFI funding, the Right inadvertently pushed the federal government to create the NFPF and to shift the nation's preservation priorities to orphan films. Since 1997, the NFPF has been preserving a diverse multicultural and compelling cinematic record. When the Right successfully battled the National Endowment for the Arts, they could not have imagined that the federal government would cultivate, only a few years later, a more varied and broader portrait of the twentieth-century record that directly challenged the Right's singular and fixed view of culture and history. It may be the only war in history in which orphans are the battle's victors.

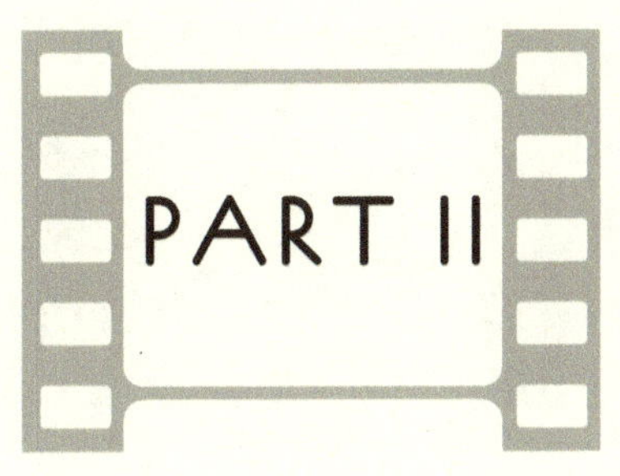

ARCHIVAL TECHNE

4

THE ARCHIVE AT THE END OF THE CENTURY

Discipline, Excess, and Access

The federal government, the public, and the film industry's investment in archives and film preservation has resulted in an abundance of historic and contemporary cinematic material flowing into moving image archives, at the beginning of the twenty-first century. This archival abundance is tempered by the fact that much of our early cinema remains missing. Jan-Christopher Horak, an influential film scholar and moving image archivist, and the current director of the UCLA Film and Television Archive describes the alarming mortality rate of early film:

> As in life, the dead outnumber the living by a long shot. Although we have only just celebrated the first century of cinema, the statistics of mortality are frightening. Of all the films produced during the silent era, i.e. between 1895 and 1930, approximately 90% have been lost. In other words, only ten percent of all films from that era are still in existence. Of all films produced during the nitrate sound film era, i.e. between 1930 and 1955, only about 50% survive in any form. . . . Meanwhile, the negatives are lost, the remaining distribution copies are routinely destroyed or worn out through continual use. Films disappear from view and consciousness, unless some interested party manages to put a print away for safekeeping.[1]

A desire to recover the missing early twentieth-century film historical record has helped to shape the culture of the moving image archive since the early twentieth century. This drive toward recovery and completion remains a fundamental but impossible objective despite the fact that most archives are perpetually backlogged. Public archives do not have the financial resources to entirely manage their collections and archivists struggle to properly manage, conserve, and catalog archival collections. While the public moving image archives diligently work to ensure and protect the artifacts of cinematic history, the current material reality of the archive has tipped toward proliferation. With all of the filmic material flowing into the contemporary archives, present and future historians will have a plethora of artifactual evidence, but the backlogging condition creates a new condition of absence. Archives do have a relatively small collection of archival gems that they rely upon to help commemorate and acknowledge the cinematic past, but they do not have the time or the money to construct identities and cinematic meanings for most of their film material.

The Safety Room

The UCLA Film and Television Archive is a massive storehouse of mediated twentieth-century popular culture. It maintains the largest collections of media material of any university in the world and is the second largest media archive in the United States, second only to the Library of Congress. The UCLA vaults contain more than 220,000 motion pictures (5,000 of which are 16 mm) and television titles and 27 million feet of newsreel footage. Among its holdings are 35 mm collections from 20th Century Fox, Paramount, Warner Bros., Sony/Columbia, Republic, Orion, and the Hearst Metrotone News Library, as well as a substantial number of independent films from the Sundance Collection. The American Film Institute, the Academy of Motion Picture Arts and Sciences, the Directors Guild of America, and the Stanford Theatre Foundation (as well as hundreds of predominant individuals, such as Rock Hudson, William Wyler, Stanley Kramer, Tony Curtis, Hal Ashby, and Jean Renoir) have donated films to the UCLA Film and Television Archive. It also has a vast collection of television programming, such as the entire run of *The Jack Benny Program*, *The Smothers Brothers Comedy Hour*, *The Carol Burnett Show*, *Hallmark Hall of Fame*, *All in the Family*, and the *Mary Tyler Moore Show*, and over forty years of Emmy Awards broadcasts (as well as all the nominated programs). In addition, the archive holds more than ten thousand television commercials.

A latecomer to the archiving community, the UCLA Film and Television Archive, established in 1969 without collections or financial support, was originally named the National Television Archive. The archive's collections grew slowly and somewhat unconventionally in its early years as its second director (and former dean of the UCLA School of Theater, Film, and Television) Robert Rosen explains:

> A typical acquisition might take the form of a midnight caravan of student-owned cars and Volkswagen buses racing to the rescue of a mountain of nitrate prints stacked on a studio loading dock awaiting imminent deposit in the "ocean vault" off the Pacific coast. A typical storage area in the earliest days was a private garage or a decrepit turn-of-the-century vault in downtown Los Angeles paid for by friends of the archive or the curator. Film inspection and repair were in the hands of a small, irregularly compensated staff, assisted by dozens of earnest undergraduates in Bob Epstein's curatorship class. Access to the growing collection was limited to a single Steen beck viewer housed in a closet in the film school and occasional screenings at the handful of campus or community theaters equipped to project nitrate.[2]

While the UCLA archive's beginnings were humble, it has always been geographically privileged. With the other big film archives on the East Coast, it was uniquely situated on the West Coast and a heartbeat away from Hollywood. Perhaps the largest advantage of being situated in Los Angeles is the ease with which the archive has been able to acquire holdings from collectors who have worked in the film industry and have lived in close proximity to the archive. With the hiring of Robert Gitt in 1977, the UCLA Film and Television Archive was poised to become an international leader in film preservation. Building its holdings, reputation, and exemplary staff during the 1980s and 1990s, its dynamic growth has paralleled that of the United States archiving community.

In his book about the preservation of memory in the eleventh century, Patrick Geary suggests that in part, history is the material practice of sorting and containing the past. He claims that "how one stores the past affects what is remembered, and thus that a change in the storage causes change in the content. The two are inseparable."[3] If Geary's assertion is correct, then the UCLA Film and Television Archive's safety room is not only an exemplary metaphor for understanding how contemporary archivists confront archival moving image materials, it is also indicative of the labyrinthine process that future researchers will have to undergo to understand the past.

A massive inventory project, the safety room is where film donations are piled until they are inventoried. Some have been waiting to be processed since the late 1970s and 1980s. There was a sense of organization that led me to believe that someone who worked there could find almost anything with only a little trouble. Jennifer Teely and Todd Wiener, both archivists at UCLA, explained that the sometimes decades-long inventory backlog was a result of a lack of manpower, prioritization, and the archive's inability to control the flow of donations and deposits. When depositors secure their materials with the archive, they retain ownership but the archive has the right to make transfers, preserve the materials, and make them available for educational purposes, classroom screenings, and scholarly research. Donors sign over ownership to the archive, enabling the archive to use the materials more freely.

As with many nonprofit organizations, the workload at the archive exceeds available staffing. Without enough archivists to manage the inventory, prioritization and the inability to control the rate of donations and deposits become larger stumbling blocks. Sometimes the acquisitions are enormous, and when they are perceived as substantially superior in quality to other inventory, Teely and Wiener must stop what they are doing and immediately attend to the new material. "We don't control the opportunities that we have to collect items," Teely said. "Someone might approach us with a collection that they want to donate, and it might be a very valuable collection and they want to get rid of it quickly because they are paying rent on it in another storage facility and they want to bequeath it to us. If we want it, we have to take it right away. We can't say, 'Can we take it a few months from now because we might have more time later to deal with it?'" The UCLA archive received Mel Torme's film collection containing 800 to 900 film titles—approximately 3,000 reels—a medium-sized acquisition. Torme's widow wanted to move the collection immediately; thus, the archive acquired the collection without the necessary preparation time.

While spatial logistics may not be the first thing that comes to mind when considering acquisitions, Teely asserted that simply finding a space for a film collection is a critical part of the process. "We had to move everything around to make space for this sizable collection," Wiener said, "because she had to have it out of the house to sell it."

Wiener and Teely assured me that in theory they want to get all the materials inventoried and processed, but they have little control over the flow of acquisition priorities. At times the donors and depositors simply need to move the materials because of their own life circumstances. At other times, priorities are created by way of donor relationships with the archive. For instance, UCLA's relationship with the Harold Lloyd estate means the archive works to accommodate the estate's needs whenever possible. "We have a huge relationship with the Harold Lloyd estate, and we recently acquired another major acquisition from them. It's the third or fourth one we've received from them," Wiener explained. "This becomes a priority; as in 'You should do this soon.' And then other acquisitions logically become less of a priority."

As I toured the safety room, I wondered how a researcher might access any of the material that was not yet inventoried. Much of the room seemed to be a massive accumulation of matter without identity; until the films were processed and logged into a database, they seemed nonexistent entities. Wiener acknowledged that the materials could not be accessed by way of an outside database but emphasized the process of backlogging. "It is not that it has been stuck in the room and forgotten and no one knows it is there," he explained. "I don't know if you saw ALL the Turner boxes stored in the safety room. It's the Turner library: the old MGM movies; the old Warner movies, on 16 mm because that's how they used to screen these movies on TV. I don't know how many titles that included, but it's thousands and thousands. When that came in (that was way before Jennifer or I got here), they inventoried all of the titles, so we have access to that backlog. If a researcher wants an obscure title, and it is not in our regular database, we can go into the backlog databases. We know it is there; we just have to take a few extra steps to find the title."

Backlogging is both a systematic process for an overwhelming amount of material and an effective metaphor for the archival process of acquisition. The nearly overwhelming matter within the safety room is not necessarily a problem for the UCLA archive, but it represents the breathtaking abundance of contemporary moving image material currently filling safety rooms and vaults across the United States. As we have seen, in the early twentieth–century, archivists actively sought out cinematic material so to save the history of motion pictures; today archivists are reeling from the amount of material they must try to manage. The stopgap process of backlogging suggests both archival diligence and ineffectuality, and is suggestive of the present-day archival dilemma: simply accounting for all of the acquired matter so someday someone might massage it into history.

Much of the material in the UCLA safety room is not a mystery to the cinematic world; a high percentage of the filmic matter stacked in the safety room is duplicated elsewhere—cataloged and stored in other archives and viewed and written about by scholars and the public. As Wiener explained archival acquisition is not a pick-and-choose process. The UCLA archive acquires entire collections; many of the films currently stored in the safety room are not enormously valuable because they are duplications in various formats of existing and popular titles. But amongst those titles are others that have potential and significant cultural and cinematic value. They often lie dormant awaiting attention from an archivist who will eventually move both the promising and not so promising material beyond its backlogging status into a catalog system.

The safety room's abundant stockpile is a clear measure of the archive's status as an important site for donors and depositors. The purpose of the UCLA archive, like other moving image archives across the United States and the rest of the world, is to be a protector of cinematic heritage. Like a foster parent who cares for many children but does not call any of them her own, the archive is the guardian of its holdings, usually without the claim of ownership. Studios and individuals who deposit or donate films are not financially responsible for the films once they are in an archive's care. While recent collaborative relationships between studios and archives have resulted in financial alliances for the restoration of some films, this has not been the norm historically. Archives, for example, are responsible for storage costs. These costs include the price of real estate required to maintain optimum storage conditions for film collections. Other costs include cataloging, care, transfer, maintenance, and for some films, restoration and preservation.

Attempting to manage and keep track of acquisitions, deposits, donations, and copyright ownership is also part of the custodial work. Similar to finding a film in the backlogging system, ownership clarification can be complicated, for at times there is a labyrinthine route one must follow to determine the status of film ownership and copyright. The historical and contemporary mergers and divisions of film companies can sometimes create complications in understanding which studio or individual owns a film or maintains copyright status. Discussing the Paramount collection, for example, Weiner attempted to explain the intricacies of its ownership status. He said that the Paramount nitrate films were gifted; Teely replied that she thought they were on deposit. "Well, the Republic titles are on deposit," Wiener stated. "It's interesting. I think the Paramount nitrate was gifted to us and the rights are held by Universal. I think half are donated and half are deposits. Because you look at some of those titles up in ORION and it says 'gifted' or there is no acquisition on that field, there is no deposit. There is no donation. That is a kind of acquisition *unknown*." They assured me that it was not a standard collection such as the Warner Bros. collection, which Warner Bros. has always controlled. "It is interesting," Wiener explained, "because Universal is allowed to access early Paramount titles because they own the rights. So, there is a kind of Father, Son, and Holy Ghost relationship. So who knows?"

Archives manage the material nature of films as well as their more abstract properties—such as keeping track of the Paramount acquisition's deposit and donation status. While ownership of copyright is an important part of a film's biographical information, much of the significance of the donation/deposit and copyright status within the archive is linked to what is permissible to do with the film. Wiener acknowledged, for example, that many of the studios have deposited nitrate prints. "We have the Fox studio prints of a lot of their early musicals and noir films, and we have a lot of Warner Bros. nitrate and a lot of Paramount nitrate. The Paramount is kind of an interesting collection in itself because the studio still controls the material. Let's say we get a request for that material to be screened, to be programmed to the public. We don't control that material, so the studio needs to contact us and say, 'Yes it is OK to loan the material to this individual or to this institution.'"

Teely reiterated the difference between physical ownership and copyright ownership. "You always have to remember that if a film is physically owned by UCLA, the archive is able to control the material to a certain extent. However, that is not to say that we necessarily have the rights to that material," she stated. "A lot of our time is spent contacting rights holders to see if they approve a venue screening or whatever. Just because we have something donated to us, we still don't hold the rights."

When an archive does hold the copyright to moving image material, it has the potential to profit from it. Essentially this is the only situation in which cinematic material has the possibility of bringing in money. Owning the copyright for moving image material means there may be financial benefit because it can be utilized commercially. The UCLA archive, for example, owns the copyright for the Hearst Metrotone newsreels, a collection of twenty-seven million feet of film from the 1910s to the 1970s. The Hearst Corporation donated the Metrotone collection in the 1980s. Eddie Richmond, former director of the UCLA archive, explained that because they own the copyright, the archive can screen the materials publicly, make it available for research, and can also license it. Licensing of the newsreels (which generates 95 percent of the commercial income for the archive) brings $500,000 to $600,000 in annual income. But most filmic matter drains the archive of its financial resources.

The UCLA Film and Television Archive and other nonprofit archives, of course, do not have a commercial mission; rather their primary aim is to protect and cultivate cinematic and other visual heritage. The UCLA archive is part of an institution of higher learning and one of its chief aims is educational access, so while the financial outlay of deposited material is enormous, the rights to use it for educational purposes seem to override, at least philosophically, the financial drain. As part of the UCLA Film and Television Archive deposit agreement, deposited materials may be used by the archive for "classroom and research screenings on the premises of UCLA for which no admission is charged, but may not exhibit the Materials publicly or allow them to be used for any commercial purpose without prior written permission from Depositor." Wiener explained that a deposit's main benefit is that it can be used for educational purposes on the UCLA campus: "We can use the material for classroom screenings and for researchers. There are individuals at the screening room now; they are researchers who are doing books or articles or they are programming a series on so-and-so so they want to see all of their films. I mean, you have to have a legitimate reason to show up here and watch a movie, you can't just show up and say, 'I really feel like seeing Bette Davis in Blah-Blah-Blah.' But, as part of the deposit agreement, we have access to the material as an educational device, so that's a huge benefit right there," Wiener said. The materiality of the safety room suggests archival wealth, but a powerful archival undercurrent is scarcity and desire to compensate for what have been lost. Archival anxiety both pushes and shapes the practice of acquisition, sometimes creating material excess. In a backlogging state, the proliferation of moving images ensures a wealth of material for future history making, but it also has the potential to choke the current archiving system making it difficult to account for the matter within it. As we have seen, it is not always even clear who owns the material within the archive, as is the case of the Paramount nitrate films.

When cinematic materials are not within the Hollywood realm there is generally much less information about the materials. Independent, regional, and amateur films, for example, usually come to the archive with much less contextual information than studio films. Without context (what is on the film? who filmed it? where did they film it and when? why did they film it?) moving images within the archive remain mostly unknowable. In the archive, they are secure, as they won't disappear or be thrown away, nor will they fall into the hands of collectors who are not interested in making them available to researchers. But they are not entirely accounted for either. The backlogging of cinematic material creates a new kind of filmic mystery. There is security in knowing that the cinematic materials are being physically cared for, but this condition does not relieve biographical anxiety. Without an accounting, without classification and biographical information, the cinematic material stored in an archive has little visibility. Until an archive can construct frameworks of meaning, moving images are merely celluloid matter that requires care and maintenance. Cinematic abundance suggests potential for the writing of future histories, but most unidentified film cannot speak for itself. Filmic material cannot reach its potential for history making until its biography unfolds.

The Biography of Film: Creating Value

Jane Johnson Otto is the Media and Music Metadata Librarian at Rutgers, the architect and developer of the National Science Foundation–funded Moving Image Collections portal, and the Getty Foundation–funded Women Artist Archives National Database. She was also a cataloging librarian at the UCLA Film and Television Archive for seventeen years.

Much of her professional life has been focused on accounting for moving image material, and at present she is recognized as the United States' leading expert in moving image cataloging. Her professional perspective reflects the most current and well-considered ideas about cataloging. When I spoke to Otto about the significance of cataloging she suggested that it was the least understood but arguably the most important element of archival work. It is least understood, in part, because it is a "behind the scenes activity." Accounting for moving image material is arguably less glamorous than restoring it. The signatory labor of film restoration is visible because it is viewed, acknowledged, and perhaps commended by other archivists and the general public, but the cataloger's labor is not generally acknowledged in film culture. The public, for example, may sit in a theater and relish the work done by well-regarded film restorationists, such as UCLA's Robert Gitt or Ross Lipman, but it is unlikely that anyone except other catalogers or a few researchers ever celebrate cataloging work.

However, it is the cataloger who recuperates and constructs cinematic biographies. Interestingly, cataloging that moves beyond description and is researched by catalogers is called *authority work*. It is the labor of disciplining the scattered and making the unseen visible. "I would argue that cataloging is actually the foundation of archiving in some ways," Otto explained, "because if you don't have description of materials, you can't preserve it; you can't show it to the public, you can't exhibit it; you can't give it to researchers. And without authority work, it wouldn't be accessible." Otto explained that cataloging is the "process of creating and then systematically arranging the records that comprehensively describe the materials held by the institution." Both the description and the arrangement are designed to facilitate search and retrieval for research, programming, acquisition, circulation, preservation, rights management and other management functions. At UCLA, catalogers try to watch the film material they are cataloging because the title frames are considered to be the definitive credit. Otto explained, "Basically we are considering the film itself as the definitive source, so we describe the film: giving the title, the distribution information, who distributed, where and when. The description would include headings for people, places, related works, and topical subjects. We put some of the major production credits like the director, the production company, and then we put places, if it took place in a particular place, we would put the place name."

This practical approach to cataloging is necessary at UCLA due to the lack of staff and the amount of material that flows into the archive. With hundreds of moving image materials arriving each month, it is impossible to conduct the research necessary to create substantial authority work and the thorough biographical information necessary for the creation of value for each artifact. Otto detailed an example of the complex and time-intensive work that is required for one Hearst Metrotone news story entitled "Behind the Scenes with Metrotone." The opening intertitle, she explained, read: "Here's how a Broadway Show is whipped into shape." The story is about a rehearsal for *Strike Up the Band* (1927). Because George Gershwin is pictured and it is his production, Gershwin is indexed. It is also indexed as a musical review, a newsreel, and short. Behind each of those headings is an authority record. Otto explained that when the initial search was enacted, it was discovered that there were twelve records on Gershwin and there was already an authority record. A cataloger cited the work on which the heading is based, and then cited the sources where she got the cross-references. "You have to keep in mind too," Otto emphasized, "that there is an international audience, so there are transliterations and various forms of names. So for every heading that's on the record, that work has been done." Otto said that a short newsreel is much less complicated to catalog than a feature film that might have a cast of twenty. Indexing focuses on prominently displayed names and notable people. If there is a minor credit that is buried, but it is a person perceived as significant, that too is indexed.

Otto stressed that without this kind of cataloging information there is simply no way into the catalog and no way into the collection. And because of the constant flood of materials into the archive and a small staff that is not capable of managing all the material, catalogers, like the archivists who manage the physicality of the collections, are routinely forced to make decisions and prioritize their labor. At UCLA cataloging priority focuses upon preservation materials and licensable footage. "We tend to put the preservation materials up at the top because we figure we are preserving them because they are important and because people are going to seek them out because they know we have preserved them," Otto explained. "We have a high profile preservation program so it is likely people are going to search for those materials."

Archival decisions about what filmic matter is considered important enough to preserve and restore has a strong influence upon cataloging decisions. The material deemed as most significant receives the most attention by catalogers; thus, the most prominent artifacts become even more visible. Well-detailed biographical information, the authority work, helps to boost the value of materials that are already constructed as culturally meaningful and significant within archiving culture. The priorities of the archive, coupled with a lack of time and staff support, create a cataloging condition whereby the most valued and prominent materials are boosted into the limelight by way of biographical detail. This process benefits the visibility of the material deemed significant and helps to enhance the reputation of an archive. On the other hand, a great deal of the moving image material within any archive remains unknowable. Without the necessary *authority* work, with only a skeleton of a biography, filmic matter can be likened to Sleeping Beauty. Until a prince (or princess) of a cataloger gives it an identity, it is only celluloid matter snoozing away in a vault.

Acquiring and accounting for moving image material at UCLA may seem breathtaking in its scope, but in relative terms, it is entirely manageable compared to the amount of material that archivists and catalogers at the Library of Congress confront each working day. The Library of Congress is the oldest federal cultural institution in the United States, the research arm of Congress, and the largest library in the world. According to James Billington, the Librarian of Congress, the mission of the library is "to make its resources available and useful to the Congress and the American people and to sustain and preserve a universal collection of knowledge and creativity for future generations."[4] The library receives approximately 22,000 items (books, printed materials, recordings, photographs, maps, music items, and moving images) and adds 10,000 items to the library collection *each working day*. Because the library is home to the United States Copyright office, the majority of the collections are received through the copyright registration process. The largest and most all-inclusive collection of American and foreign films and television broadcasts in the world, in 2009 there were 1,213,180 items in the library's moving image collection.[5]

"We are just buried under so much material," laments Arlene Balansky, a moving image cataloger at the Library of Congress. A librarian since the late 1970s, Balansky describes the library's moving image collection as eclectic. "I actually like the variety of material that we get, but the downside of that, since we are getting a lot of material through copyright deposit on a monthly basis, we get buried under it. And we also get a lot of very large gifts and sometimes purchases, with the idea that 'you don't want to pass this up.' But how do you make it accessible to people?" Catalogers, according to Balansky, do not have the time to view the moving image materials that come to the library, making it impossible to analyze them in any detail. Even copyright materials may not have complete biographies because claimants do not always finish the registration process, Balansky explained.

> If we are going to spend time solving mysteries, it is likely to be older material. It's the nitrate film that has come in without titles and credits. Sometimes I have to identify it. Now that used to be something that we worked on more. Then we went through quite a long hiatus where we really didn't do much preservation material. I think people made the decision because they were buried by copyright material, and they had to move it out and deal with it. We are struggling with how to deal with that in an expeditious way, so we can deal with the gift material and the donated material, which includes nitrate and other materials, avant-garde materials, things like that.

Approximately 90 percent of the moving image cataloging records at the library has a minimum of information; Balansky characterized the records as "low level cataloging." Because catalogers do not have time to do authority work on most of the materials that come to the library, Balansky explained that a two-sentence summary might be the most a researcher can reasonably hope for when they search for information. She emphasized that it is often researchers, not catalogers or other employees at the library, who unravel the mysteries of the library's moving image materials. Employing their tenacity and investigative skills, researchers help to construct the identities of moving image material by shaping their biographies, thereby developing the cultural and social significance of some of the artifacts in the collection.

"When it is something major, like *Citizen Kane*," Balansky said, "we don't need someone to come in from the outside to tell us what's important to preserve or to find in a vast collection." At UCLA, catalogers give priority to cinematic materials that the archive has preserved or will preserve—materials that have already been deemed by the archive as culturally significant. It is often the case that the materials with an already stable identity receive the most attention and their biographies continue to grow.

At the Library of Congress the situation is similar. Careful attention is paid to moving image documents that are already culturally constructed as historically relevant. Such materials are readily accessible to researchers, making it fairly easy for researchers to work with materials. Their investigations add more to the biographies of well considered moving image materials, helping to further develop and maintain their cultural significance. As a result, the informational imbalance within the archive perpetuates itself. Matter that is already deemed important circulates easily—helping to reify its meaning. Material that lacks identification tends to remain a mystery.

Much of the historic materials in the library's moving image collections are essentially unidentified. However, while archivists, catalogers, or researchers have not yet constructed its cultural significance and have not unraveled its mysteries, it is still understood as valuable within the culture of the archive. Its worth lies in its *potential* for cultural meaning. While much of the material within a moving image archive like UCLA or the Library of Congress lies dormant and it overwhelms those who must tend to it, on most days the archiving community does not wish for it to disappear. Generally, moving images with scant identity and little constructed meaning are viewed as cultural objects in waiting. It is not clear if or why they are important, for they cannot speak for themselves; however, in their latent state, there is hope that someone someday will come along and discover its potential.

Paul Spehr, a longtime and well-known archivist and onetime assistant chief at the Library of Congress, articulated his version of this archival hope when we spoke. He remembered that in the 1970s, there was great concern within the culture of the Library of Congress about the rapidly growing moving image collection:

> They said, 'Well, you shouldn't select so many films. Limit how many you have.' And we said, 'what standards do you apply to selecting materials? How do you know what somebody is going to want fifty years from now?' We saw the first wave of scholars that came in here. They were not interested at looking at Hollywood films as Hollywood films. The first one coming in on a regular basis was Tom Crooks who was looking for how blacks were being treated in film. He didn't want to see *Citizen Kane*. He'd seen it. He wanted to see other ones. We'd seen one wave after another of people coming in *not* looking

for the exceptional but for the ordinary. So, we swept everything we could in here.

Spehr emphasized that as academics began studying films as part of their research agenda in the 1970s, the library staff quickly concluded that acquiring moving images that represented cinematic artistry would not be enough. Spehr and his colleagues recognized that researchers wanted to look at films in the library's collections because they could access the history of the twentieth century by way of moving images. Acknowledging that as an archivist he "cut his teeth" on the paper print collection, Spehr suggested that the nonfictional elements of the collection shaped his acquisition philosophy. "My example of the value of film is to take a camera outside on Independence Avenue and film the people walking up and down the street," Spehr stated. "If you took a look at this today, you'd say, 'oh it's not too interesting.' But put that footage in a can for 300 years and then see how interesting it is. A good bit more interesting than *Citizen Kane.*"

Spehr certainly does not discount the historical significance of popular Hollywood film, but he suggests that the nonfictional world recorded on film has the potential to be extremely relevant to researchers as they write the histories of the twentieth and twenty-first centuries. Spehr explained that the library's acquisition philosophy has been viewed as being quite broad in its approach because the Library of Congress and the researchers who come there have placed great value on the moving image documentation of daily life and the cultural and social worlds captured on film. "We knew film was about society and about how people lived," Spehr explained. "We never wanted to turn anything away."

Spehr, like many other archivists with whom I have spoken, offered an example of why turning away or throwing away moving images is never a good idea. He recounted the time when the network ABC, which had never registered any of their soap operas, registered all of them—all at once. "In this room," Spehr remembered, "there were shelves from one end to the other with *General Hospital* and *Days of our Lives.*" Spehr thought one of his colleagues was going to have an "apoplexy" when he saw the room stacked with soap operas. "I thought he was going to die," Spehr told me. "He wanted to get rid of them. I said, 'No. Keep them!' He tried to get rid of them, but he couldn't because it is very hard to throw out. It's much easier to put it in a box somewhere." Spehr said that ultimately the soap operas were easy to organize because they were single titles and week by week broadcasts. "If you have it lined up properly," he explained, "you don't have to go through it and say so and so is in love with such and such and this kind of thing. It organizes itself." Within six months of the soap operas being nearly thrown away, researchers from Germany, who were funded by Volkswagen, came to the library to study American soap operas. "So you just never know?" I asked, when he was finished telling me the soap opera tale. He nodded and said, "If you can keep it all, you should keep it all. I would buy a big salt mine somewhere and put it all away in there. Films are pouring in here. Why not keep it?"

The scarcity paradigm developed in early twentieth-century archival culture persists. Archivists, like Spehr, are driven to collect and acquire as many moving images as their institutions will allow. There does not seem to be a limit to what they desire to collect. During much of the twentieth century, archivists were predominantly concerned with recovering what remained of the cinematic past. Because of their alarm over what had been lost, they developed a compulsion to collect cinematic remains. This compulsion to amass persists into the twenty-first century; however, in our current culture, archival accumulation has led to an outcome that goes beyond recovering filmic relics that reflect the formation of a new art form. As Spehr suggested, almost all past and present moving images have the potential to be culturally significant, to someone and at some point in time.

The fundamental difference between archivists fifty years ago and today is their view of time. Moving image archivists, historically, focused their vision upon the past; they mostly looked in the rearview mirror. Contemporary archivists look both backwards and forwards in time. They too wish to recover the past, but they are also focused on the future. They acquire and collect moving images so to fill the gaps of cinematic history, but they also desire to obtain and protect present-day filmic matter because someone someday may find it significant and useful.

Most archivists imagine the moving image researcher who will be working in the mid-twenty-first century. Generally, they conjure up this imagined future researcher by claiming that they have no idea what will be important to her; so almost all moving images should be collected and protected. The contemporary archival manifesto is based upon a temporal view that stretches both backward and forward, resulting in an abundant accumulation of matter. It is, in fact, a surplus that is not easily managed. We might call it an overstock of moving image materials that exist with little or no identification. While backlogged moving image materials are protected within the archive, they are hidden nonetheless. The archival anxiety of yesteryear remains, but it has been transformed. Iris Barry and her colleagues lamented the destruction and disregard of early cinema. Today archivists lament the fact that they are buried under an excess of material. Both are certain kinds of death.

In the archive, death is never far away. During the last century, great care and effort have been taken to collect and create value and meaning for filmic representations of the dead. Today, the moving image archive stores the potential for reanimating the dead, but the avalanches of material bury many of the promises and possibilities of communicating and connecting with those who lived before us. Perhaps an important lesson has not yet been learned. At this time, archival forecasters are already imagining their own deaths. Desiring to please later generations, desiring to explain *us* to *them*, they accumulate massive amounts of material. But, like a message in a bottle in the vast ocean, the possibilities of contact with the future are slim. Salt mines and hard drives of moving images surely suggest the potential for knowledge and communicating with the dead, but avalanches of material may bury many of the possibilities for future contact.

Making Contact

Historically, the moving image archive has had a reputation for acquiring what was considered to be significant materials and then locking them away in the vault. Some archives, more privatized than the Library of Congress or UCLA, were secretive about their collections, protecting the identities of some of their valued artifacts, even from other archivists. This reputation for secrecy and inaccessibility has lessened a great deal during the last few decades. Moving image researchers with whom I have spoken express their frustrations of not being able to gain access to archival moving images because of parsimonious copyright holders who seem a little too enamored with the power they have over their materials housed in the archive. As we have seen, significant amounts of archival material have little biographical identification; without catalog information it is impossible for researchers to know moving image materials exist. They cannot bemoan their lack of access to materials of which they are not aware. In my experience, it is archivists, rather than researchers, who fret the most about accessibility. Their concerns about managing the materials exceed the overwhelming amounts of work they face, for the contemporary archivist is trained not only to consider the images of which she is the custodian, she is also educated to care about sharing moving images with the public. This causes anxiety in the archive, as if there were not enough already.

The Museum of Modern Art was a primary and foundational institution for the collecting and archiving of moving images in the United States. Founded in 1935 as the Film Library (now called Film and Media) the collection now includes more than 22,000 films and four million film stills. While part of Barry's purpose for collecting films was to archive the origins of a uniquely American art form, today the department of Film and Media has the strongest international film collection in the United States. Among their holdings are the original negatives of the Biograph and Edison companies and the world's largest collection of D. W. Griffith films. The Circulating Film and Video program has more than 1,200 16 mm prints that are accessible for viewing. The circulating film and video program construct a particular history of film from the 1890s to the present.

Unlike UCLA and the Library of Congress, the film and media department at MoMA is not a part of a university nor a library, but rather a department within a museum of twentieth-century art. Of course, universities, libraries, and museums all share a mission of providing information and resources to various publics, but the aim of museums in general is exhibition—the arrangement and display of collections. When I spoke to Anne Marrow, a curator at MoMA, she helped put into perspective the relationship between the department of Film and Media and the rest of the Museum of Modern Art. She explained that very few museums in the world have a film department. At MoMA, she said, film is an equal partner. "We privilege film as an art form by saying it is equal to photography, painting and sculpture," Marrow explained. "I think by the sheer fact that it has been recognized by the museum as a significant art form gives it that special quality." Marrow explained that the museum has no interest in the fact that film is a commercial enterprise where lots of money is at stake. "We continue to focus on the beauty of the works, their importance in film history, what they mean in terms of movements in technology," she explained. "That's how we keep the works special, even though they are mass-produced."

Marrow explained that the museum has three interrelated missions. It recognizes itself as an educational institution, first and foremost. Its exhibition program, for which it is best known, arises from its educational mission, and the collections are, of course, the materials that are exhibited for the purpose of educating the public about art and culture. "These three parts all work together, and when you have a collection you have to have conservation," Marrow explained. "Everything becomes the great branches of the tree, and we are very much focused on the public mission." With the museum's focus on education and exhibition, public accessibility to the film collection is of great interest and concern to those who work in the department. Mary Lea Bandy, retired chief curator of Film and Media at MoMA, views public exhibition as an integral part of film preservation. "A film is preserved after its elements have been made and its exhibition prints have been made and the film is shown again on a screen. And after you show that film to the public," Bandy contends, "then you can consider that you have completed the preservation of that film. Preservation is not preserving a film and locking it up in a vault."

Film is a distinctive art form at MoMA because of its history as a mass-produced, duplicative, public art. Bandy and Higgins reiterated film's unique identity explaining that films are distinctive, because they do not hang on the wall and darkness is required for their exhibition. "We are viewed totally differently (from the rest of the departments)," explained Bandy. "Our works are not insured. They are not kept. They are not handled, cataloged by the main areas of the museum that work on all of the collections." Higgins differentiated between film and other art at the museum: "For me the distinction has always been that we are the art form that exists in time as well as space," he stated, "which is another way of saying that we are a performing art." This, in part, is why Bandy and Higgins both consider public exhibition to be an integral element of film preservation at MoMA.

"Film preservation involves not just the object but the presentation of the object," Bandy said. "Our thrust of the museum's expansion project is to provide our theaters with the kind of viewing conditions that still present film on a large scale, as close as possible in the way that it was originally presented." The Film and Media staff aims to preserve both filmic matter and the cinematic experience. The restoration and preservation of cinematic material is theoretically complex, but it is not as an abstract endeavor as preserving an *experience*. For the MoMA staff, film preservation includes safeguarding the act of moviegoing; making contact, in other words, is part of how they define preservation.

Both Bandy and Higgins reject the contemporary filmic experience of singular viewing on small screens. "Films were meant to be seen with audiences. They were not meant to be seen in isolation or on a little wristwatch," Bandy said. "I am not interested in seeing a film miniaturized. I want to see film as *film*. Perhaps, someday soon, only museums and archives will provide screening conditions that approximate the way the films were originally shown. Films may become chiefly a museum experience." When I spoke with Bandy and Higgins, the museum's theater space was temporarily housed at the Gramercy Theater in Manhattan while construction and restoration of the museum were underway, but today, two state-of-the-art theaters, with a total of six hundred seats are open at the museum, with approximately twelve thousand annual screenings taking place in the Roy and Niuta Titus Theaters. The Titus Theaters are entirely contemporary in design, with upgraded digital surround sound and projections systems. While Bandy and Higgins may be nostalgic for the cinematic audience, they are not nostalgic for the architecture of the filmic experience. "We are not trying to recreate the nickelodeon or the cathedral cinema experience," Higgins explained, "but we are trying to recreate the sense of a communal experience in a theater with other human beings, reacting to the rhythms of what is on the screen, as a group, that's the cinema experience."

The nature of the film medium is inherently different than most of the museum's collections, helping to highlight the issues and obstacles of accessibility. The popular view of cinema and its mass production can lead to frustration for curators and archivists, as well as those who wish to gain access to the museum's film collection. Historically, moviegoing has been a public experience. For much of the twentieth century, cinema was exhibited widely; simultaneously, in cities and towns across the United States, hundreds if not thousands of people watched films together every day. Its public nature, along with its mass production and distribution, has helped to create a perception that films should be easily accessible. Other mass-produced artworks in the museum do not share cinema's public personae. It is unlikely, for example, that anyone in the general public would consider borrowing the museum's Josef Hoffmann Sitzmaschine Chair. While the Sitzmaschine was mass-produced, its form cannot be replicated in the same way that a film can because in film's inherent nature lays its potential for duplication. In addition, the experience of a chair is a private experience, while cinema has been a public one.

"Sometimes I get someone calling quite enthusiastically from either a high school or an organization requesting a film. But we worry about our materials, and when we've determined that their projection skills are less than stellar we won't lend the materials to them," Marrow said. "And sometimes people will respond by saying, 'Well what is the good of the material in your vault, if no one can see it?'" Marrow sympathizes with their perspective, as she explained that she does not wish to limit access to film materials. Most contemporary archivists, Marrow said, believe that if films can be handled responsibly and with care, access should be given. Historically, access has been strictly limited; archivists believed every time a film is run through a projector, it has the potential to be harmed.

"If the film can be treated respectfully and responsibly then in fact the world should see it. But I still deal with people who call, and I have to say, 'No we can't lend something or you know, it's unique in our collection.'" Marrow explained that the Film and Media department only lends films that have been preserved. If a film in the collection only exists as a single print, it can be shown on the museum premises but it will not be lent for public viewing. Marrow explained the tension that arises as a result of conflicting archival desires. "Let's use *Run Rabbit Run*, for example. All we have is that print, so if someone called us and asked to borrow it, we would say 'No' because we don't have a negative for it," Marrow explained. "The likelihood of having a negative for a contemporary film is slim to none. So people will then say, why do you have it then? It belongs to the public. Well, I don't disagree with that, but the sheer fact that we have treated it in such a very special way means that it exists. Somewhere down the road everything in the collection can be preserved, but you have to be responsible until that point; to not let things out, and so, that does in a way, hinder our exhibition."

This conflict is not unique to the film collection at the Museum of Modern Art. The push to publicly exhibit films and the pull of protecting film materials is a tension that contemporary archivists consistently face. Most archivists have a great desire to show the films within their collection; however, they resist exhibiting some materials because they are trained as archivists to protect film material. Archivists are wary to exhibit a film if they do not have its negative, if it has not been preserved, or if there are not multiple prints because film is compromised each time it is handled and run through a projector. The preservation of a film is a costly and time-consuming process that requires both skill and artistry. Few archives manage to preserve more than a dozen or so films a year; thus, most films in most archival collections are not exhibited or accessible to the public.

A film that is deemed culturally and historically significant gets priority treatment within the archive and is likely to gain easier access to the film preservation queue. Once a film has been preserved, it often garners attention by the archival community, and it is more likely to be circulated, exhibited, and celebrated within the public sphere. If a film was not publicly recognized as significant before its preservation, it is likely that it will be after its preservation, due in part, to its increased exposure. Films deemed important by the archive circulate more easily, helping to reify their cultural and historical meanings. Films that have not yet been considered for preservation tend to remain obscure and unseen.

While other archives have their own theaters and offer regular screenings to the public, the museum's function as a place of exhibition helps to illuminate the potential relationship between preserved films and the public. Few other archivists and curators with whom I spoke emphasized the importance of making contact with audiences and recreating the cinematic experience in the way that Steven Higgins and Bandy did. The museum has around 1,200 annual screenings. Approximately half of them expose audiences to earlier twentieth-century cinema. The museum's earnest exhibitory mission is remarkable, but there are far more films at the museum than there are opportunities to exhibit them.

The Memory and History Feedback Loop

Exhibition is integral to an archival gem's meanings. A showcase film brings with it already constructed meanings and a sense of completion, but audience members often re-enchant the film with their own memories and meanings. It is this exhibitory process that transforms archival films into objects of popular memory. The archival film *From Stump to Ship*, for example, is a canonical amateur film preserved by Northeast Historic Film (NHF), a regional moving image archive in Bucksport, Maine. NHF's mission focuses upon the collection, restoration, and exhibition of New England's nontheatrical moving images. The archive's founders, David Weiss and Karan Sheldon, are widely recognized as innovators and leaders in the moving image archival field. As I have discussed elsewhere, their discovery and restoration of *From Stump to Ship* in the mid-1980s, helped to re-enchant the film as well as construct their vision for the Northeast Historic Film archive.

Alfred Ames, the president of the Machias Lumber Company in Washington County, Maine, made the 16 mm film in 1929–30. Documenting the ending of his family's long lumber business, Ames created a cinematic record of the lumber industry in Maine. The film details the daily life of woodsmen and river drivers: it shows them cutting down trees, transporting logs to the river, driving them down the river, and finally transforming them into lumber at the mill before the load is shipped to Boston. Ames created a detailed record of the woodsmen life in the early twentieth century that leaves us with a populist social history of life in the woods.

In the mid-1980s, with support and funding from the Maine Humanities Council, Sheldon, Weiss, and two scholars from the University of Maine took turns traveling across the state of Maine exhibiting the restored *From Stump to Ship*. They screened the film twenty-two times to nearly eight thousand Maine residents, over a period of five months. In the town of Machias, eight hundred people viewed *From Stump to Ship*, a staggering number considering the town has a population that hovers near two thousand residents. At each screening, the film was introduced by a scholar. The historian David Smith spoke at the *From Stump to Ship* premiere at the University of Maine on September 20, 1985. He detailed the filmmaker and the film's biographical information, but he also spoke about populist social history and how films such as *From Stump to Ship* enable contemporary people to view a world lost by the passing of time.

The film, then, was framed from the onset as a significant restored artifact. Audiences were told why the filmmaker, the film, and its restoration were important to the state of Maine. In this way, *From Stump to Ship* was presented to audiences as a disciplined archival artifact. But at the moment of exhibition, the film was re-enchanted by the audience members. Engaging with the contents of the film, audiences added new layers of meaning to the ones already carefully constructed by the archive.

Reflecting on the film's presentation in Blue Hill, Maine, Sheldon describes how some of the film's viewers connected with the film. "At seven o'clock there were people in every seat and lining the walls. Mrs. Tapley said that she remembered the *Lucy Evelyn* [the schooner in the film] unloading coal in Blue Hill—her father was a coal merchant," Sheldon wrote in her screening journal. "One of the first people to arrive was Newt Grindle who grew up in North Blue Hill. At the age of five, he was at the other end of a crosscut saw from his father. They had oxen and used them to haul and bring the logs to town. I asked if there were a lot of people cutting at the time, and he said he counted 28 pairs of oxen one day." At the Presque Isle exhibition, Sheldon remembers that four river drivers came to the viewing. "After the presentation many people stayed in the cafeteria for molasses cookies. The river drivers stayed and told stories endlessly," Sheldon wrote in her journal after the event. "Vern [one of the woodsmen] was away in the woods and came home to find a new daughter. 'Where did you get that?' he asked his wife. He'd been gone six months or more."

The scholarly contributions to the project and the presentations substantiated the fact that the film and the woods life depicted in it were valued and historically significant. However, the voices of the men and the women who had lived the woods life provided more credibility to each presentation. After the film's exhibition, audience members spoke to the film, sharing their memories of woods life. More casual conversations also ensued after the film presentations. Sharing their memories and expertise of the woods life, friends, family, and members of the community were able to provide witness to woodsmen's compelling stories and memories. Except for well-known figures, such public remembrance is a rarity. The archival film, then, became a vehicle for Maine residents to remember a principal way of life that has all but disappeared from their state. *From Stump to Ship* has an official identity as a recovered and restored film, and when Maine audiences encounter the film, they use its sanctioned history as a platform for recovering and illuminating their personal memories. Their stories, in turn, enrich the film's sanctioned meanings. This process is what enables the film's history to be dynamic and a part of popular culture.

Conclusion

Many cultural critics and historiographers agree that we live in a time of accelerated history because many of the past social structures that once sustained cultural memory have disappeared. Attempting to reconfigure and restore memories that have not been sustained over time, social groups living in postindustrialized communities construct and re-construct a multitude of complex, diverse, and creative tributes, memorials, museums, statues, archives, historic sites, and television, radio, and film programming to what they cannot, or fear they will not, remember. The United States is an accelerated archival country, in part because there is cultural consensus that if we do not collect, classify, store, catalog, and sometimes exhibit our remains, the tethers to the past will be at risk of being perilously broken.

Pierre Nora explains that collective memory began to falter when peasant culture, "that quintessential repository of collective memory whose vogue as an object of historical study coincided with the heyday of industrial expansion," disappeared.[6] Furthermore, Nora states that the cultural institutions that sustain ideology, memory, and cultural values no longer function in a manner that allows for a smooth transition from past to present. When cultural-ideological institutions stop functioning in a way that binds the past to the here and now, history steps in. While contemporary culture is busy and fascinated with the pathways it paves to the past, some current historiographers imagine that we create an odd dream of the past.

History, John Lewis Gaddis asserts, is not reality and, "if truth be told it's a pitiful approximation of a reality that, even with the greatest skill on the part of historian, would seem very strange to anyone who'd actually lived through it."[7] Gaddis explains that the predominant problem with the fragmented representations of historical realities is that they eventually replace the memories of the people who have experienced it firsthand. "We make the past legible," Gaddis claims, "but in doing so we lock it up in a prison from which there's neither escape nor ransom nor appeal."[8] Gaddis finds some solace in the fact that historians contest interpretations of the past because conflicting histories allows for expansive historical thinking. By allowing for competing viewpoints, historians are "showing that the meaning of history isn't fixed when the making of history—and even the writing of history—is finished."[9]

History is "the reconstruction, always problematic and incomplete, of what is no longer" and memory is "always a phenomenon of the present, a bond tying us to the eternal present," Nora explains.[10] He argues that memory "is," while history is a fuzzy and incomplete representation of the past. While the archive may attempt to regulate and discipline the meanings of a film, at the point of reception, sanctioned cultural implications can give way to more personal appropriations and manipulations, which can then feed back into its historical representations. History and memory, in other words, can be imagined as existing together in a feedback loop, rather than existing on opposite sides of a spectrum. Memory and history, in the archive, can comfortably exist together, intermingling rather than being in diametrical opposition.

During most of the twentieth century, archivists and scholars believed that the primary obstacle in the construction of film history-making was the lack of artifactual evidence. In the future, however, the composers of the cinematic record may face a different sort of challenge. Despite an inundation of material evidence in archives, if archives persist in a backlogging state, future historians, like their counterparts before them, will also face an impoverished record. While parts of the cinematic twentieth century have been corralled into sanctioned narratives, the glut of moving images will necessarily prevent archivists, historians, and researchers from comfortably taming the past into history. The past, as it currently exists in the moving image archive, is not a willing, sleeping maiden waiting patiently for the scholar to transform it into history; it does not exist as a continuous chain of causes and effects that exist in a homogenous time-space continuum. Historic intention struggles to pave a narrow linear path, but it is almost always imperceptible. Both the overwhelming inundation of archival moving images and the public's re-enchantment of archival films help to create the conditions that resist historicism, enabling the mysteries, the collisions, and tangled cinematic stories to persist like stubborn weeds.

The current conspicuous accumulation of film within archives may itself eventually become part of the history of cinema. As future scholars look back at history making at the end of the twentieth century, might they be just as interested in the film archive's excess as the materials collected within it? Might archival proliferation tell them as much or more about the century's end as the films collected? When considering the work of the collector, Walter Benjamin writes, "Perhaps the most deeply hidden motive of the person who collects can be described this way: he takes up the struggle against dispersion. Right from the start, the great collector is struck by the confusion, by the scatter in which the things of the world are found."[11] Our celluloid fortresses that protect us from forgetting are also symbols of our desire to contain the scatter of twentieth-century experience.

5

FILM RESTORATION

A New Way of Seeing Film History

Most of an archive's labor and its budget are expended in the supervision and protection of its materials. The amassing, sorting, cataloging, and caring for collections can be likened to the efforts required to keep a domicile in order; it goes largely unnoticed by anyone other than the people attending to it. While it is true that film archives gain and maintain their reputations, in part, by the size, quality, and kind of collections they hold, the restoration and public premiere of a film can bring recognition and acclaim to the archive, as well as to film restorationists. Though the restoration of a film deemed historically and culturally significant is valuable for film fans, cinema scholars, and the archival community, relatively few films, per year, get entirely restored. Film restoration is an expensive and labor-intensive pursuit that requires technical skill, artistry, detective work, and a deep knowledge of the cinematic past.

This chapter is an investigation of what film restorationists do and how they think and talk about their work. Current restoration discourse and practices literally assemble and help to shape cinematic history and reveal how the moving image archive influences the ways that a film history is understood. Focusing on several film restoration case studies, in-depth interviews I conducted with some of the country's foremost film restorationists, and the analysis of restoration commentary on the DVD version of *Lost Horizon,* my aim is not to critique the current methods of film restoration, but to interpret the way restorationists and the archival community both conceptualize film restoration and practice the piecing together of history. This knowledge helps us to better understand how restorationists regard the cinematic object as historical artifact and how the contemporary culture of the archive engages its relationship with the past. The work of restorationists—their particular kind of film-remaking—show us the trench work of re-constructing cinematic history. The restored film should be understood as a new type of film born from the cinematic and archival sensibilities at the turn of the twenty-first century. Well-regarded by scholars and the public alike, the restoration film follows the same filmmaking principles as other kinds of cinema, but its promise to audiences is unique.

Contemporary restoration discourse offers us an alternative to traditional ways of constructing film history. The general aim of film restoration tends toward reconstructing the first chapter of a film's existence, but restorationists resist a singular path of history making. Keeping their eyes on the moment of a film's premiere, restorationists also attend to a film's multiple histories: its theatrical release, its alterations and cuttings, its fall into obscurity, its neglect, as well as its previous imperfect restorations. Restoration not only resists singularity, it also privileges what is not known about a film's history and highlights the creative and imaginative work that is required to piece history together.

"We can use the past fruitfully only when we realize that to inherit is also to transform," David Lowenthal articulately argues. "What our predecessors have left us deserves respect, but a patrimony simply preserved becomes an intolerable burden; the past is best used by being domesticated—and by our accepting and rejoicing that we do so."[1] The current discourse of film restorationists is a model for history making because it makes transparent the ways that a history is spliced together; it reveals that stories of the past are transformed by those who aim to recuperate them, and it leaves the door open for further historical interpretations.

Film Decay and Cinematic Remains

While almost all matter used in the creation of art, be it stone, canvas, plaster, wood, metal, or paper, tends toward attrition by way of the elements of time and nature, human erosion, or mishandling, film stock is particularly vulnerable. I can think of no other artistic enterprise that is so expensive to produce and is so fragile. It might be perceived as a great misfortune and an irony as well that cinema, one of the world's most well received and greatly loved forms of entertainment and art, is incredibly delicate in its composition. Other variables, such as the fervent disregard and disposal of films, have contributed to cinematic loss during the twentieth century, but decomposition is a leading factor in film's disappearance from the heritage map.

Until the middle of the twentieth century, films were produced using cellulose nitrate, a chemically unstable film stock. Cellulose nitrate was manufactured using cotton linters that reacted with nitric and sulfuric acids. The polymer was then dissolved in chemicals, so to improve the polymer's properties, and cast on a polished flat bed, which produced a layer of polymer in solution. Residual solvents then evaporated, leaving a thin plastic film. Cellulose nitrate is highly combustible, which is a big problem as nitrate film ages and decomposes. Nitrate film is exothermic, meaning that it generates heat during deterioration. If the heat produced during deterioration cannot be conducted to the environment quickly enough, then localized heating causes the film to deteriorate faster and at the same time generates more heat, which leads to further decomposition and even worse the possibility of extremely dangerous fires. Anthony Slide, in his book *Nitrate Won't Wait,* documents some of the most famous nitrate fires of the twentieth century. For example, a 1981 fire at a Hollywood storage vault destroyed 150 film reels belonging to the Academy of Motion Picture Arts and Sciences. As a result of the fire, the academy began storing its remaining nitrate holdings in the vaults of the UCLA Film and Television Archive.

Nitrate film is plagued with other destructive tendencies besides its highly flammable nature. Left in its can, without proper temperature and humidity controls, it deteriorates. During the first stages of decomposition, it becomes brittle and shrinks; its images fade and become discolored. Without intervention, decomposition continues and nitrate film becomes soft and gummy. If the process is not retarded, it becomes a brown sticky liquid. Archivists call it "honey." This liquid then solidifies, and in its ultimate state of decomposition, reddish brown dust is all that remains.

Because of the hazards of nitrate film, in the late 1940s, the motion picture industry abandoned it and began using acetate film, often referred to as "safety" film because it does not have the potentially volatile qualities of nitrate film. Because acetate was believed to be much more stable in nature, the use of safety film seemed like a good alternative film stock and a giant step forward for the preservation of nitrate films. Unfortunately, stored cans of acetate also decompose to a state archivists call "vinegar syndrome," due to the rank vinegar odor caused during deterioration. Films suffering from vinegar syndrome not only smell bad but also experience shrinkage, brittleness, and degradation of the film image. Bleaching of the film image can occur even when the film stock appears to be in good condition. With proper archival conditions, vinegar syndrome can be delayed significantly. In the 1950s, Kodak began selling polyester safety film. The strongest and most chemically stable of the film bases, it was the film stock of choice for new 35 mm films produced in the United States. Because it is more durable, it can better withstand projection mishandling than acetate or nitrate.

The nature of film stock, then, is quite vulnerable to disintegration, but mechanical damage and the mishandling of film also contribute to the loss of filmic material. Anyone who has viewed an older film that has not been restored has seen the evidence of such maltreatment. The dust, dirt, and scratches that mar the film's images are a result of worn rollers, incorrect threading into the projector, improper shipping, or working with the film on a dirty surface. Molds and mildews can also damage a film's emulsion if it is stored in humid conditions. Once these biological agents have eaten into the emulsion, there is little that can be done to recuperate the image loss. Finally, a film's sound is also vulnerable. Acetate films with magnetic sound tracks are particularly susceptible to vinegar syndrome; archivists believe that the iron oxide in the magnetic track may act as a catalyst for decay. When a film with vinegar syndrome shrinks, the magnetic strip is degraded. In the worst cases, the magnetic coating may completely separate from the film base.

The historical inventory has also been debased by routine disposal of films during the early twentieth century. The migration of films to private film collectors and foreign archives has also made obtaining information about films or parts of films more difficult for the signature work of an archive. Other circumstances that compromise the filmic record are the deliberate cutting of a film by censorship boards or studios that produced the film prior to its release; the shortening of a film on release or re-release; the cutting of sexual situations, violence, or portrayals of racism; the cutting of some pieces of a film for re-sale or re-use; and the removal of some parts of a film by a private collector, who acquired a film illegally and wishes to conceal the identity of the film. Other hazards to the cinematic historical record include such natural disasters as the June 2008 Universal Studios back lot stage fire. Besides destroying the *Back to the Future* set and a *King Kong* exhibit, the fire raged through a vault, containing forty thousand videos and film reels. Nearly all of the archival prints stored in the vault were destroyed. According to Universal Studios, the films' elements still exist, but it is likely that only the biggest titles will ever be reprinted or seen again on 35 mm film.

Nonetheless, the compositional nature of film has surely been one of the greatest challenges for contemporary archives. The cultural shift from cinematic negligence to filmic preservation, along with the science and technology that have enhanced the ways archives care for their collections have helped to build a sturdier dam against the ever-growing bulk of cinematic material. However, restorationists and preservationists continue to confront many complications caused by past cultural neglect and the lack of information and awareness about decomposition and the retarding of it.

The Case of *Molly O'*

Film restoration has become a familiar term in DVD marketing. A "newly restored" film is a successful marketing technique for motion picture studios. While studios are increasingly committed to what the archival community currently views as a more complete and authentic film restoration, a newly restored film may only mean that the studio did a digital clean-up of the film, made a new print, and perhaps added a few scenes that the director originally omitted from the film. This is not what well-regarded film preservationists within the archiving community consider restoration. The film preservationist's aim is to physically work with, reconstruct, and ultimately protect the film's original elements. To restore and protect a film in this way requires working with other archives across the world to find particular elements of the film that are missing or damaged, physically handling the film, and using current technology. Restorationists employ technological skill, historical methods, and creative thinking to restore a film—a process that often takes years.

To understand what an archival film preservation project entails and the principles that guide it, let us first consider the restoration of the film, *Molly O'*. A silent romantic comedy, with overtones of class-consciousness and tension, this 1921 film was produced by Mack Sennett and directed by F. Richard Jones. *Molly O'* was made in the United States and starred Mabel Normand, who made her name at Keystone Studios and was an established star prior to Charlie Chaplin coming to Keystone. Normand made some forty feature films and directed Chaplin in several of them. Today, six of those films survive, but most of the six are incomplete.

Jere Guildin, a UCLA archivist, directed the restoration. He explained that at the beginning of the *Molly O'* project, the UCLA Film and Television Archive had only a five-minute section of the film, preserved in the early 1990s. Guildin said there was a rumor within the archival community that Gosfilmofond, the Moscow film archive, had a complete version of *Molly O'*. Gosfilmofond has had a reputation of holding United States silent films, according to Guildin, without making them readily accessible to United States archivists. They did not give or lend UCLA the *Molly O'* negative, but Gosfilmofond did give UCLA a fine-grain positive master copy made from their negative. The fine grain positive, an intermediate element, enabled the UCLA archive to make a duplicate negative (dupe negative) of the film.

After UCLA made a dupe negative from the fine grain, Guildin greatly anticipated seeing *Molly O'* in its entirety, but when he began watching it, the first hurdle to the film's restoration was immediately transparent: the intertitles were in Russian. A mainstay of the silent film era and a significant key to many silent films' narrative logic, intertitles convey character dialogue and advance the film's narrative; Guildin was going to have to find a translator or an original script or synopsis of the film before he could progress with the restoration. Fortunately, he found the title lists and the synopsis at the Margaret Herrick Library; this Beverly Hills institution probably holds the most complete collections of film-related materials in the world, including nine thousand screenplay scripts in various stages of completion.

As he read the English intertitles and plot synopsis, Guildin discovered another hurdle; the Russian fine-grain master was far from complete. On the positive side, the Russian intertitles would not need translation. "We didn't have to translate anything from Russian," he explained to me. "Thank goodness because many of the intertitles are joke titles. Trying to translate humor from other languages doesn't always work out too well." But the beginning of *Molly O'* was missing, and Guildin suspected other scenes were missing as well.

> It didn't dawn on me after I read the synopsis and obtained the footage of the first seven minutes that all of the comedy sequences in the movie had been cut out. There's an opening slapstick comedy sequence right in the beginning of the movie that is missing from the Russian material. In fact, the way that it was edited you have no idea that was missing. Frequently there is someone taking a pratfall. Molly trips at one point and falls over. At first when we got the material I thought they were unfortunate splices because you see her start to stumble and then you see her standing. So you never see her take the comic spill. We joked that over in Russia since all of the comedy was cut out they called this *The Plight of the Poor Irish Washer Woman in America* and made an entirely different movie out of it.

In reconstructing the intertitles, Guildin used the five-minute section of *Molly O'* that UCLA preserved in the early nineties. As it had the original English intertitles, Guildin could re-create the original intertitles' font. He also inserted the five-minute preserved section into the restored film because its quality was better than the Russian material. Having discovered the whereabouts of the first seven minutes of the film, Guildin was able to obtain the footage from a private United States company. This provided the original main titles and the first five-minute comedy sequence missing from the Russian print. Guildin could not find any of the other comedy sequences, but he added the five-minute comedy sequence, he explained, so viewers could see a sampling of the kind of humor that existed in the original film. Using stills, the synopsis, and the title list, Guildin was able to bridge many of the sequences that were missing from the film. "Sometimes," he said, "I just used titles saying: 'here is what happened.' And other times, if we had a fair amount of stills, I tried to reconstruct a little bit of the missing sequence using the dialogue. If we had a still of Mabel Normand

and someone else talking, I cut between their head shots and brought out a little bit of the dialogue, so you can get an appreciation for what the scene might once have been."

Using character headshots and cutting between them to reconstruct missing film sequences is a contemporary practice used by well-regarded restorationists in the archival community. Guildin admits that inserting photographs and stills into a motion picture can be disconcerting to the viewer. "After *Molly O'* was shown there were many people that liked it," he said, "but some didn't appreciate the use of stills and intertitles with dialogue because it slowed down the film. We were doing a reconstruction and we were trying to make it as entertaining as possible without, you know, I used the bits of dialogue that I thought were pertinent, and didn't try to go whole hog in re-creating everything because we couldn't and it really would have been boring. I used the synopsis up to a point where I thought dramatically it would work, cutting between stills and headshots."

Filling in the visual, audio, and narrative gaps requires research, speculation, and imagination. What remains of the original film (in all of its various forms of originality) is key to the completeness of a restored film, but for films that have been considered culturally significant for one reason or another, there are likely to be other elements to help reduce the uncertainty about a film's missing parts: written documentation such as screen plays, journals, press releases, advertising material, and photographs taken on and off the set are cataloged in archives and libraries. Sometimes, people involved in the original film are available to explain what they remember about the making of the film. And of course, restorationists glean much information about the films they are restoring from the knowledge within the archival community.

Restorationists do find contextual information about lesser-known works, but there is likely to be much less documented and researchable information. The contextual information and what remains of the film helps to reduce conjecture, but restoration still requires a certain degree of speculation and imagination. Inserting stills and headshots into a film when original scenes are missing is an accepted conventional practice for filling in the visual and narrative gaps created by a missing scene. Aiming to reinstate an incomplete film's visual and narrative logic, restorationists construct a semblance that suggests many dimensions of an original and complete film. The re-created scene, in other words, is informed speculation on the part of the restorationist and bridges the more complete sections that remain of a particular film.

Filling the narrative and visual gaps helps move the restored film toward completion and enables viewers to more closely experience the film's original intention, as it is understood by the restorationist. But it is also a cinematic disruption that changes a film's meaning. Eileen Bowser, the influential curator of film at the Museum of Modern Art who wrote a seminal essay on film restoration in 1990, admits that such insertions in a restored film are inelegant but necessary. "Such insertions are awkward and disruptive of the viewer's enjoyment," she writes, "but to ignore the missing scenes is misleading."[2]

The continuity of the soundtrack with the insertion of the still photographs interrupts the temporal and spatial flow of the cinematic experience. While this convention may help viewers have a better sense of the missing parts, it also helps to highlight the film's breach. A reconstructed scene is a narrative and visual solution, but it challenges a film's continuity and serves as a visual reminder of the archival effort. "The objections of some viewers to these devices is understandable," Bowser admits. "The classic Hollywood cinema is based on the spectator's unconscious acceptance of an illusory reality. Anything that tends to break that dream-like illusion is resented. Nevertheless, we think that the function of a film archive is to make as clear as we can what the original version was."[3] The reconstructed scene resists the temporal flow of *Molly O'*, which Guildin describes as an experience of *slowing down*. A rupture and its remedy are abrupt reminders that modern people have employed studied technological and creative efforts toward preserving the idea of an original version of a film that once existed.

The restored film should be considered a new *type* of film. In other words, while the reconstructed *Molly O'* works toward replicating the 1921 film, it is valuable to consider the restoration film as a unique cinematic form, born within a particular cultural logic during the interregnum of the twentieth and twenty-first centuries. Through this lens, we can see that the splicing of filmic remains creates a viewing experience of both continuity and discontinuity; the restored *Molly O'* is composed of a five-minute segment preserved by UCLA, a seven-minute segment obtained from a private company, an incomplete Russian print without the Russian intertitles, new reconstructed intertitles, and reconstructed sequences created by integrating stills and new dialogue intertitles. The restored film follows most of the fundamental principles of cinema. The material and conceptual essence of film is its modifiability; thus, the restoration film, with its various insertions and additions, logically aligns with the traditional and fundamental principles of cinema and filmmaking. The restorative method of juxtaposing disparate elements and recreating missing scenes by inserting stills is, in part, an attempt to reinstate and smooth out the 1921 narrative.

Yet its distinctions from other cinematic forms are important to consider as we situate the restored film within the culture of the archive. A restoration fills in gaps, creating a more cohesive and complete cinematic narrative, but in the process of reconstruction a new filmic narrative is created, one that helps to define and distinguish the restoration film from most other kinds of films. The restored film, first and foremost, offers viewers a unique promise, that of bringing the spectator closer to the *idea* of the film's first viewing. As we have seen, the restored film's essence is its remains, remnants of what cameras recorded in the past. The restored film promises to bring viewers in close range of the past by splicing together the most intact remains of the original film.

The restored film, then, is indebted to the past, but unlike the restoration of other art forms, it deviates from the idea that restoration references a particular artifact. Restorations of buildings, paintings, sculptures, or even graphic art are usually considered in reference to an original or its remains. Judged in relation to what is known of the original, restorations are rarely considered without a comparison: how true to the artist's original intent, artistry, palate, and workmanship is the restored piece? These kinds of questions suggest that the quality of restoration work is defined by its ability to be authentic to the original artifact. A good restoration is judged so because it precisely aligns with the materiality of an artifact. However, questions of the authenticity of the artifact itself are not generally part of restoration critique. The material authenticity of *that* building, *that* painting, *that* sculpture is rarely in question.

Films are different though. When Walter Benjamin was considering the cultural implications of authenticity in an age of mass production, he pointed to the singular event or the material object: the choral production, the painting, and the cathedral. Perhaps he would be surprised in the ways the contemporary culture has bestowed the notion of authenticity to the mass-produced cinematic form. Mechanical reproduction—a world of copies—creates a desire and value for the original work. When it comes to film, the attempt to replicate the conditions of an original is at work in such phenomena as the director's cut or a film's premier. Things become complicated when we look toward film as having a comparable sense of an "original" work as in, say, a painting or sculpture. Moving image restoration moves away from the cultural belief that restoration references an original singular artifact. The *original* film is not a material object; rather, it is a conceptualization of an artifact. To be specific: it is an idea of a film that existed prior to its first projection. The well-known archivist Paolo Cherchi Usai thoughtfully describes this theoretical first moment: "This hypothetical condition can be defined as a potential moving image. Once it has been projected, the film resulting from this intention is subject to the physical decay of its images and the memory of perfection is lost, thus giving birth to the history of cinema."[4]

While we may imagine and theorize a film's first moment, restorationists rely upon what remains of camera negatives and information about the film's premiere. This is their path toward determining a film's origins. In some cases there is no camera negative, or like in the case of the *Molly O'*, it is incomplete. In the silent era, the usual practice was to have six or seven cameras filming at the same time, challenging the idea of *a* camera negative. And modifications also came quite early in the career of a film, as studios and censorship boards routinely adapted them to better suit their purposes.

The value of a restored film is judged differently than other kinds of films and restorations. With its own peculiar reference backwards, its authenticity is judged by its resemblance to a mass-produced artifact conceptualized in a singular moment in time. Unlike other kinds of films, the restored film is not judged by its cinematic content, but by how well it aligns with dominant interpretations of the film's past. Principal film conservators are quite aware of the abstract nature of their work and some worry that the hypothetical nature of their translations can stretch the parameters of logic.

Peter Williamson, who has been working in the archival field since 1979 and was the film conservator at the Museum of Modern Art when I interviewed him, explained that in the pursuit of excellence, some restorationists simply go overboard. Exacerbating this phenomenon is the fact that duplicate negatives were not made before 1930. "You had multiple cameras going side by side," Williams explained, "or else you had the same camera going and you said, 'Alright, take one is the American; take two is the British; take three is the French. Let's try to get them right, and let's hope the best take is the domestic country's negative.'" Such prints are beneficial when archives search for missing scenes or to insert footage that has been damaged, but according to Williamson, when people begin picking and choosing the scenes they like the best, the restoration project becomes corrupt.

"You've now got people saying, 'Well, this shot is really better in this source.' 'Oh, and I like that little gesture which isn't in the others, so we'll use the Portuguese shot.' What we are finding is that restorationists are literally stitching together new versions of films," Williamson explained. "And they are being advertised as 'this is the way it was originally.' Well, it was never seen in that version by anybody, at any time in the history of the planet, before whatever the date is when you unveil the restoration. I think it is going to come back and bite us." Williamson imagines future scholars and archivists will be highly critical of such restoration fabrications. Or worse, they will not be aware that they are fabrications at all.

Restoring *Mr. Smith Goes to Washington*

One of the principle aims of current film restoration is to create and renovate an environment that replicates past filmic experiences. The restoration film addresses disparate audiences separated by generations. Eileen Bowser argues that film restoration's most important goal is to create the film seen by its first audiences. "To understand an old film, we try to get into the skin of those who saw it in its time. The film as it was shown for the first time is the goal of all our restoration projects at the Museum of Modern Art. We are not always able to reach it, but we get as close as we can."[5] Embedded within the cultural meanings of the restored film is the promise that viewers will have a similar cinematic experience as audiences that came before. Part of the experience and likely the pleasure of watching a restored film is an acute awareness of this temporal disparity; the restored film promises to level the differences and bring the past to contemporary (and future) viewers. However, the Herculean attempt to bridge the temporal and experiential gap between present-day spectators and the film's first audiences also serves to highlight the illusive, distant nature of the past.

Part of the experience for contemporary viewers of film noir era, suggests Slavoj Zizek, is an awareness of temporal difference. Today's viewers of film noir are fascinated, he explains, with the mythic naïve gaze of a film's initial audiences. Because they are divided between fascination and ironic distance, they are not entirely absorbed by a film noir's narrative.[6] Whether original audiences of film noir were completely captivated by the narrative is uncertain, but as Zizek suggests, the recognition that the images the camera recorded were intended for another audience, an entirely different generation of moviegoers, creates a unique cinematic experience.

David Francis, the retired chief of the Motion Picture, Broadcasting and Recorded Sound Division at the Library of Congress explains that moving image restoration should aim for a close representation of the filmmaker's intention. "It is a determination of the original form prior to copying," Francis writes, "and the reconstruction of the work from a multitude of sources." This definition, of course, focuses on the artifact, the materiality of the film. But, when I spoke with Ken Weissman, head of the Motion Picture Conservation Center at the Library of Congress, he explained that Francis brought a view of archiving to the United States that extends beyond material preservation. "David brought with him the European view, which I think was a little bit ahead of the American view at the time," Weissman explained, "that access was important. With regard to film archives, you want to preserve and make the images accessible, but you want to preserve the experience of cinema as well, so you want to be able to have a film print that you can show." Part of the contemporary archival impulse, then, is to not only help to restore films but film environments as well.

When I interviewed Weissman, he detailed the Library of Congress's restoration of Frank Capra's 1939 film *Mr. Smith Goes to Washington*. One of the library's first restorations, Weissman explained that the impetus for the project came from David W. Packard who pledged financial support for preservation and restoration of a number of Capra films. Packard, who has a particular interest in classic narrative films, is a primary benefactor of moving image restoration in the United States and has helped to guide film restoration at both the library and UCLA.[7]

Before the work on *Mr. Smith Goes to Washington* that began in 1989 and finished in 1992, the Library of Congress had only done, what Weissman calls, mini-restorations. Weissman recalled that the focus of the library's film laboratory during its first seven or eight years was simply to preserve cinematic fragments. "If you have two prints of a film that are both incomplete, and yet you are still missing a big section of that film, well, there is no point of cutting together what you can cut together, just copy and preserve what you've got, and who knows, maybe in five years down the line, you'll get another copy that has the rest of it, and then you can finish the restoration. So you want to be in a position where you have preserved the content of what you have."

But Weissman explained that the library's early approach was not the only archival method that used to be practiced in the United States. "Let's say you've got a roll of film, a short film, a one reeler," Weissman offered as an example, "and you have two prints on it. And one print is complete except part of the film is deteriorated, let's say the last fifty feet of the film, is really not viewable any longer, and you have another print, that isn't complete, but you have that last fifty feet intact." One approach, he explained, is to splice them together, making a complete roll and then copy it. "That's certainly a valid way to approach a project," stated Weissman. "However, in some ways, it tends to violate what professional conservators look at as a valid approach because under the first guise of 'do no harm' well, if you are cutting one piece of film and inserting it to another, you can't say you haven't done harm, at least to that one piece of film."

While most archives do not currently practice restoration this way, Weissman understands the impetus behind the splicing tradition. "You have multiple frames and things have to be intact or they don't work. There's not much point if you have, for example, a film that was originally six reels and all you have is two reels of it. It's not good as a film anymore," he stated. "It may be good as an artifact, and maybe you can conserve it as an artifact, but as a film it doesn't exist."

Distinguishing between an artifact and a film, Weissman highlights the two driving forces of the moving image archive—the preservation of materiality and that of its first audiences' experience of it. The artifact is valuable whether or not it is complete, but the artifact must exist in its (imagined) entirety in order to best re-create the historical experience of the film. The distinction between the artifact and the aesthetic experience of the unified whole is not unique to cinema.

Theorists of restoration, as we have seen, have wrangled with the definition of unity and how best to come close to reconstructing it. Cesare Brandi, for example, argued in the 1960s that restoration could replenish an artistic object's unity that had been fragmented by time, interference, and alteration. But the parts had to be put back together in order to recuperate the original aesthetic experience. He writes, "The fact remains that, once mosaic tesserae and stone blocks have been dismantled from the formal arrangement imposed upon them by the artist, they remain inert and do not preserve any effective record of the unity of which the artist has made them a part. It is like reading words in a dictionary; those same words that a poet has arranged in a verse, and that once separated from the verse, become again nothing more than a group of semantic sounds."[8]

The aesthetic experience of a restored work of art, Brandi suggests, can best be experienced by way of reunification. Weissman's distinction between cinematic artifact and film indicates a similar view; the cinematic artifact exists as potential for re-creating the film in its entirety. A restored film sometimes offers contemporary viewers an aesthetic experience that resembles a film viewed by its earliest audiences. Unlike most artistic restorations, the filmic reconstruction can be complicated by a superfluity of fragments of varying quality. As we have seen, restorationists aim to bring a film back to its original state, but as Weissman explained, that can be complicated by the fact of multiple premieres. "In many cases there was a premiere version, but then shortly after, a few select markets, like New York and Los Angeles had premieres, and then the film went out to the rest of the country," Weissman stated. "In order to get one more screening in a day, distributors might cut five minutes in lesser markets."

When Weissman began the *Mr. Smith Goes to Washington* restoration he discovered six different versions of the film with six different running times ranging from 119 minutes to 130. Through research of early documents, such as scripts and reviews, he ascertained that there were really only three different versions of the film. The 119 minute version and the

120 minute one, he concluded were probably the same film but had slightly different running times. "When do you start the stopwatch?" Weissman explained. "Do you start it when the curtain pulls back or do you start it when you see the first frame? That can make the difference."

But the biggest obstacle for the *Mr. Smith Goes to Washington* restoration was that one of the film's key scenes was missing from the original negative. Weissman described the problematic three-minute scene, "I believe it was the very beginning of physical reel three. Smith arrives in Washington by train. He gets out and he kind of looks off and he sees something and he walks toward it. And from that point on, he gets on a bus, and then it goes through a very complex montage of scenes around Washington DC. You see the Tomb of the Unknown Soldier; you see the Capitol; you see the Lincoln Memorial; and you see him walking up and looking at Lincoln. I think it was the first time the cinematographer used this technique in his career, so, it was considered a signature thing and it was missing."

In 1959, twenty years after the original premiere, restoration work was apparently done on the film. Though Weissman does not know who did the work, he speculates that it was done for a twenty-year anniversary of the film. Unfortunately, for the library's restoration, 300 feet of one reel had been replaced with a 16 mm duplicate negative in 1959. This section of the film had either been removed prior to 1959, Weissman speculated, or it was severely damaged and they removed it at the time of the 1959 restoration. "We don't know what happened to it, but it was gone, and it was replaced by a duplicate negative that was blown up from a 16 mm print. They had actually physically taken it out of the original negative," Weissman said with alarm. "Almost three minutes of the film. When this thing came onto the screen it was like someone stuck you in the eye with a short stick. It looked positively awful."

The restoration of the three-minute scene was accomplished by using the film's fine-grain master. Fine-grain film is used mainly for duplicating work, in the preparation of a dupe negative, where sharp detail is of the essence. It is not meant for projection on a theater screen; however, the fine-grain three-minute scene was far better than the 16 mm blowup. "We identified what could be best printed from the original negative and what could be best printed if we made a duplicate negative from this fine grain. We made a fine grain from the original negative and we made a duplicate negative from that fine grain," Weissman explained, "and spliced the two together and that was our restored picture." While the film required other restoration work, the reintegration of the three-minute scene was the most challenging and likely the most rewarding.

Interestingly, Weissman's account of the *Mr. Smith Goes to Washington* restoration suggests that while the definitional difference between artifact and film is based on a scale of entirety, the aesthetic quality of a film's entirety is also critical to contemporary moving image restoration. The original negative, prior to the library's restoration, was, by Weissman's account, complete, but the 1959 inserted three-minute scene looked "positively awful." Correcting this cinematic blemish, of course, helps to re-create the aesthetic experience of original audiences, but it also heightens the cinematic pleasure of contemporary audiences who confront the restored film by way of Zizek's double exposure, an awareness of another generation of audiences that have viewed the film. When most viewers of a restored film find some pleasure in the recognition that they are not the film's intended audience, they also bring to the experience their own habits of spectatorship, which rarely include narrative omissions or visual intrusions, such as the insertion of a 16 mm blowup.

One of the aims of the restored film, like almost all other sorts of films that currently circulate in the cinematic market, is to please contemporary audiences. While the archival community has objectives far wider in scope than satisfying contemporary cinema audiences, they are most definitely considered in their restoration work, for without the support of present-day audiences and their tax dollars, there would be little to no restoration work at public moving image archives. Thus, the restored film's audiences are not the only ones who take into consideration more than one generation of audiences. The restored film's creator keeps two audiences in mind—the film's original viewers and today's spectators.

Writing of the Library of Congress's restoration of *Mr. Smith Goes to Washington,* David Francis describes the restoration balancing act: "In the same way, except for archival audiences, it may be necessary to trim slightly incomplete shots or even cut out, say, two frames of damaged image or insert material in a show copy so that these technical imperfections do not interfere with modern audience's enjoyment of the film," Francis contends. "The cinema is basically an entertainment medium. In short, we have not lost the opportunity to present the film almost as it was seen originally, nor do we forget that today's audience has a different perspective from that of the moviegoers who saw *Mr. Smith Goes to Washington* in 1939."[9]

Nikolaus Wostry, the curator at Filmarchiv Austria, acknowledges that present-day audiences are considered in archival work but hopes for a day when they are more sophisticated spectators of what remains of the cinema that came before them. "Hopefully, the viewing habits of future audiences will be advanced enough so that they are willing to see not only a reconstruction as a self-contained dramatic work," Wostry writes, "but also fragments and deviant versions, the way fine art museums exhibit drafts and work in progress. Archival film programming should work toward that goal."[10] Wostry is proposing, in other words, that archivists help to train mainstream audiences to expand their habits of spectatorship to include cinematic fragments. If the general population considers filmic remnants valuable (as something other than entertainment perhaps), it is likely that archival habits would expand and change to the point where there is little distinction between the terms "artifact" and "film."

When the library's restoration of *Mr. Smith Goes to Washington* was complete, a premiere was held in Washington, D.C. "All of the Congressmen and Senators were invited to see it," Weissman remembered. "Unfortunately, they had a big vote that night, so many people who said they would be there, couldn't make it." Weissman acknowledged that the film's audience was "kind of like preaching to the choir," but he was quite satisfied by their reaction. "The feedback that we got back from people who were in attendance was overwhelmingly positive—from some of our own staff who hadn't seen it, as well as people from Sony who own the rights to the film—everyone was thrilled. They felt the film, though certainly not perfect, was the best seen since 1939."

"*Mr. Smith Goes to Washington* premiered in a beautiful theater, in a venue like it was supposed to be seen," Weissman said. "It was in a darkened theater with multiple people in the audience." Like most archivists with whom I have spoken, Weissman emphasized that the restored film is meant to be seen under particular viewing conditions. Specifically, it should be viewed in a movie theater, preferably one built prior to the Cineplex era. The desire of the contemporary archive is for the restored film to look as similar as possible to what audiences in original theaters saw, but the state of the modern-day movie theater, Weissman declared, makes this a difficult proposition.

He cited that contemporary movie screens are smaller and the distance between the screen and the projector tends to be much shorter than it was in earlier movie houses. "If you then go into a big movie house, like one of these restored southern movie palaces," Weissman stated, "they may hold several thousand people, and the distance and the screen and the projector, instead of being 50' long, may be 250' long. And the screen has a beautiful curtain allayed around it. The curtain doesn't just look pretty. It provides what is called a surround, around the picture." He stressed that the curtain, as well as the quality of the lens on the projector, also shapes the viewing experience. Carbon arcs, the typical projection light source for traditional movie-house projectors, are vastly different than modern-day lamp houses. "Carbon arcs are very harsh—are very high contrast light sources, which tend to give you really bold colors, or really deep blacks for black-and-white films and white whites," Weissman clarified, "but the shades of grey are more limited. They also have a different color temperature, so things look different."

In other words, the archivist has control over the restoration of the image, but has little power over its exhibition. No matter how well the artifact is brought back to its original condition, its present-day impact primarily lies in its exhibition. Theaters have changed dramatically in the last half century, and it is rare indeed for a modern-day spectator to *see* in the same manner as a restored film's original audiences. The film restorationist enters a project knowing full well that the final product will rarely look on screen as it was originally meant to appear.

A principle aim of the contemporary moving image archive is to reconstruct the artifact in such a way that contemporary audiences can see what viewers before them viewed. Moving image conservators spend years researching, documenting, and reconstructing a film so that it most closely resembles that which audiences saw at the time of its premiere (or another agreed upon origination moment). The film archive also considers the experiences of contemporary filmgoers who are a dominant consideration in the contemporary preservation equation. Archivists bring two distinct audiences separated by decades, even a century, closer together. Such a consideration enlivens the archive by making moving image preservation a social act, in part, whereby (imagined) past audiences and contemporary cinemagoers have the opportunity to mingle.

Lost Horizon

When a film is restored, the restoration process itself becomes part of what is preserved in the archive. The restoration narrative, familiar in archival and academic communities and increasingly acknowledged in popular culture, is changing the ways in which film history is understood and composed. Restoration discourse imagines a new way to understand a film's past because it considers the entire life span of a film. Traditional film histories generally focus upon a film's origins and interpret its first cultural life. But restoration discourse takes into account a film's complete biography. Rather than focusing only on its originating moments, the restoration account considers all a film's states of being, including "degraded" existences, such as despoiled network television copies. If the cultural interest in moving image restoration continues to increase during the early decades of the twenty-first century, it is possible that the restoration act and the stories about it will influence and expand the ways that cinema's history is understood by archivists, film scholars, and the moviegoing public.

"The one essential rule in all kinds of restorations," Bowser argued in 1990, "is that the restorer must let us know what has been done." She laments that it is likely that journalists and promoters will distort what the restorationist tells them, but "the restorer must write it down and, if possible, publish the history of the restoration, for the benefit of those who do have a serious interest."[11] In the last two decades, since Bowser urged conservators to document their work, the increased professionalization of the moving image archive has helped to create conditions whereby restorationists are more likely to publish written accounts of their restoration work.

At the same time, the restored film (and the idea of it) has gained currency in popular culture; therefore, it is not entirely surprising that at the turn of the twenty-first century there is some layman curiosity about the restoration process and those who do the work. The professionalization of the field and the increasing popularity of restored films have created favorable conditions for more in-depth accounts of what restorationists encounter when they go about their work. Such accounts, once they are documented, distributed, or published, become part of a film's history and part of what is being preserved at the archive.

The discussion herein has been on *what* the contemporary film restorationist is preserving when he restores a film, but the final section of this chapter focuses on the ways that a restorationist thinks and talks about a project. A cultural guide, the restoration narrative instructs its audience to see and consider the archival film as an artifact with many histories, some of them still incomplete. Central to restoration discourse is that a film's history is ongoing and that it is possible for contemporary people to have an open and enduring relationship with the past.

The audience for many published accounts of a film's restoration is the archiving community. Such narratives are written primarily to aid other restorationists in their efforts, as well as help to bring well-deserved attention to the restored film, the restorationists who worked on the film, and the archive where they work. With the increasing interest in restored films within popular culture, some restoration accounts are being disseminated for a larger audience by way of the DVD. Perhaps the most significant restoration narrative currently circulating is Robert Gitt's explanation of Capra's *Lost Horizon* restoration. The 1937 film, based on the novel by James Hilton, received mixed reviews when it premiered, and many contemporary film critics speak of it with some ambivalence. It is a story about five Westerners who flee from an Asian revolt and are hijacked and flown to the utopia of Shangri-La. While most reviewers note the exorbitant $2.5 million budget and praise the amazing scenic backgrounds and sets, they point to *Lost Horizon's* utopian focus, its lengthy monologues, and the story's lack of conflict as the reasons it is a bit long and dull.

In 1999, Columbia TriStar Home Video released the restored version of *Lost Horizon* on DVD. Significant for our purposes, the DVD includes a commentary track by Gitt and film critic Charles Champlin that runs the entire length of the film. Gitt, who works at UCLA, is perhaps the most well-known and respected restorationist of popular film in the United States. His work on *Becky Sharp* (Rouben Mamoulian, 1935), the first three-color Technicolor feature to be released, helped to put film restoration on the cultural map in the United States. Gitt explains during the commentary that while he has worked on many restorations, *Lost Horizon* is his most meaningful project and the one he has worked on the longest—twenty-five years.

Like most well-known restorations, *Lost Horizon* was a complicated project because of the many cuts and alterations made to the film over time. Capra's rough cut ran six hours, and after a test screening, it was cut to three and one-half hours. After a disastrous preview in Santa Barbara, Capra cut it down to 132 minutes for the film's premiere. Not long after the premiere, Columbia cut Capra's 132-minute version down to 118 minutes for exhibition in lesser markets. When the film was re-released during World War II, the film was cut again and changes were made to the film so to better fit the needs of Hollywood's propaganda machine during the war. As changes were made to the film over time, original footage disappeared entirely. In the 1960s, Columbia made one last print of what remained of the highly unstable original nitrate negative and gave it to the American Film Institute; the print became the basis for the film's restoration that began in 1974.

The goal of the restoration was to restore the film to the 132-minute premiere that Capra preferred (this particular originating moment is, of course, somewhat arbitrary. It might have been any one of the film's premieres). There are still photos inserted into the film's restored version, since seven minutes of the film have never been found. The current restoration incorporates a 1937 general release projection print, still photographs and freeze frames, a number of shots from a 1943 World War II fine-grain master positive, a 1950s French Canadian dubbed television copy of the film, a British Film Institute dupe negative (both a 1937 and a 1946 version), the soundtrack from the British Film Institute dupe negative, four cans of a film convention print found at the Library of Congress, which was for the purpose of promoting the film to motion picture exhibitors, and two pieces of the film removed from the film on March 17, 1937.

A full-length DVD commentary by a film restorationist is an extraordinary cultural object when we consider the indifference and, at times, resistance to film preservation during much of the twentieth century. Champlin and Gitt's 1999 commentary, similar to the director's commentary on many other DVDs, runs the entire length of *Lost Horizon*. Their running remarks have a similar cadence to television newscasters covering a two-hour live event. There are, for example, long pauses and extraneous information about the film sandwiched between Gitt's explanations of the film's restoration. Champlin speaks primarily about Capra and the actors—Ronald Colman, Jane Wyatt, Edward Everett Horton, John Howard, and George Conway—and asks Gitt questions about his restoration work on the film.

As the film begins, Gitt explains the film's troubled history and how it came to him as a restoration project in the 1970s. It is approximately eleven minutes into the film (when the main characters are on a plane unknowingly traveling to Shangri-La) that Gitt begins to instruct the viewer on the restoration process. "Incidentally, there is something very important about to happen here," Gitt says. "This sequence was one of the first ones to be cut by the studio. Right here. This sequence that you are seeing right now is an enlargement of a very grainy, very poor quality 16 mm print, which came from Canada. It was actually used for French Canadian television in the 1950s." Gitt then explains that Larry Karr at the AFI and Columbia found the scene in 1976. "This particular footage is one of the poorer looking bits of footage in the movie because there is no 35 mm, either negative or positive prints, anywhere in the world, as far as we can tell." The current poor quality of the scene was due in part to the less sophisticated lab technology available in the 1970s, when this particular 16 mm scene was enlarged to 35 mm. Gitt states he would have loved to reprint it for the restoration, but this particular sequence disappeared in 1980. "We are very suspicious that it may have been stolen," Gitt explains. "It was shipped from the west coast back to Columbia Pictures on the east coast, and somewhere en route the film disappeared and has never been seen since." Champlin exclaims, "That's amazing!"

Champlin likely found it amazing that the complex history of *Lost Horizon* includes a possible theft, but it is only one part of the remarkable narrative. To begin, Capra's production took nearly four months. Weeks after its premiere, the film began its long history of modification. At first, parts of the film were cut to accommodate the needs of exhibitors. Rural exhibitors, for example, cut the film so they could show it more times in a day. For the next forty years the film continued to be altered and more and more of it disappeared as a result. By the 1970s, *Lost Horizon* existed only as fragments of inferior quality footage, scattered across the United States,

Canada, and England. In sum, the film existed in its premiere form for a few weeks in 1937. For the next four decades *Lost Horizon* existed in many degraded variations. Gitt's quest to return *Lost Horizon* to its premiere state was a twenty-five-year effort. As Gitt's narration attests, the history of *Lost Horizon* does not end in 1937. Instead its biography has persisted for more than seven decades.

In other words, the restoration narrative challenges traditional ways of making sense of a film's history. Rather than focusing on a film's production, actors, awards, and director, the restoration narrative tells how a film continues to have a cinematic life long after its first audiences have left the theaters. It also narrates how the film was brought back to life in the cultural imagination. The restoration narrative, in fact, highlights how a film lost and found again is a significant and interesting part of its history, as are the efforts to restore it. The story of *Lost Horizon,* like most film restoration narratives, consists of three specific parts. The first part of the restoration narrative recaptures the film's significance at the moment the film premiered (it is only a moment compared to the rest of the film's history). The degradation of film is the second part of the film restoration tale. The film's mortification and corruption is explained in some detail, and if there are scoundrels to blame, they are generally the heads of motion picture studios who lacked foresight and were blind to the cultural significance of their products. The final part of the story is built on redemption—the quest to recover the film and restore it to its original condition.

The best stories, of course, are the ones in which the pursuit to recover the film is time-consuming, intellectually taxing, and technically challenging. If a restoration only requires a minor cleaning up of the soundtrack, for example, it does not merit much of a story. Only when there are mysteries that require clever and time-consuming detective work, technical wizardry, and exacting patience does the restoration and its narrative become valuable enough to share with a broader audience. The restoration tale of *Lost Horizon* is particularly noteworthy and important to interpret because Gitt is highly regarded in archival culture and much diligence, time, and creative effort were needed to restore Capra's film.

It is interesting to note that during his 132-minute commentary Gitt focuses on the parts of the restoration that he still considers substandard. The structure of his narration is constructed by way of the still-incomplete nature of the restoration, the flaws that remain in the film, and the sequences that disrupt the flow of the film and that challenge the viewers' pleasure. To be sure, it would be a dull narrative if Gitt repeatedly noted the high quality 35 mm elements of the restoration. And focusing on what the restored film still lacks can be highly instructive to the uninitiated. It is likely, for example, that if Gitt did not point to the inferior quality of the 16 mm enlargement, it might escape some spectators' attention. Gitt's emphasis on the inadequacy of the plane sequence highlights how the *Lost Horizon* footage vanished into a black hole.

Like most restoration narratives, Gitt's narrative hinges upon the gaps within the film as well as the strategies he employs to accommodate the losses, so the film can almost exist as it once did, which is to say, in its entirety at a particular point in time. Such discourse and intention mirrors the archival objectives of representing a cinematic past as completely as possible. However, John Lewis Gaddis suggests that historical knowledge is a *particular* representation of the past, made legible by the historian who both highlights and ignores various elements of what has come before. He argues that historians lay down a grid by "stifling particularity, privileging legibility, all with a view to making the past accessible for the present and the future."[12]

Like the historian, the restorationist also makes sense of the cinematic past by focusing upon and also overlooking parts of a film's past. This is not to say that the restorationist resurrects a film entirely subjectively. Rather, particular moments in a film's existence are emphasized, others are overlooked, so to construct a comprehensible restoration. The archival community, for example, most often deems a film's premiere, which generally took place in Los Angeles and New York, the original or primary version. This is an agreed-upon convention that privileges urban exhibition, but if rural exhibition was privileged instead, a film's most original form could just as well be the version that was edited for rural cinemagoers.

Once a history is constructed and accepted, Gaddis contends, alternative interpretations and particular details are swept under the rug. The past becomes comprehensible, but in the process, alternative ways of interpreting it get elbowed out, and the historical narrative becomes fixed and totalized. The aim of the archival restoration is indeed to secure a film's history—to materially fix and totalize this most frustratingly ephemeral cultural object. However, Gitt's commentary (and the film itself) suggests that the restoration process at the moving image archive opens a crack in the door for alternative and future histories of *Lost Horizon.*

Sixty minutes into the film, there is a dining room scene in Shangri-La in the restored version that utilizes both still photographs and a poor quality 16 mm sequence. Once the film returns to 35 mm, Gitt explains that he does not particularly like using stills and freeze frames. "The only alternative is for the screen to go completely black and listen to the sound track, and I think from an audience's point of view, it is better to have something visual going on, on the screen, that is related to what you are hearing and that is what I tried to do," Gitt explains. "It is not a perfect solution, but since there is no film footage that is about all we could do." Lamenting that there was no 35 mm print from which to work, making the visual quality of these scenes substandard, Gitt explains that Columbia Studios of sixty years ago did not conserve the film properly. Had the studio made protection materials and had not cut the negative and thrown pieces away, Gitt explains, "we wouldn't have these problems today."

As with many restoration narratives, the studio is primarily to blame for the fragmentation of *Lost Horizon,* but Gitt is careful to explain that it was the Columbia Studios of sixty years ago that was the culprit. The essence of film, of course, is that its pictures move, and Gitt is not particularly keen about a restored sequence that utilizes stills. Gitt is aware of his audience and the fact that the absence of motion distracts the viewer of the film, but he makes do with the stills because they are better, he tells us, than seeing nothing at all. While the stills help the viewer navigate the meaning of the scene more effectively than a black screen, they also serve as a visual reminder that parts of the past remain missing.

The most problematic scene for the film's restoration appears on the screen eighty-five minutes into *Lost Horizon,* "Here's another sequence with stills," Gitt explains. "This is actually one of the most difficult-to-find sequences in the movie because there were not even good production photos made on the set. That is why I had to use just these portraits and miscellaneous photos of the Valley of the Blue Moon and pictures of Horton and Thomas Mitchell." Gitt searched for photos of the scene, but Capra and the actors wrote it while on the set because they decided the scene could provide some comedy relief. The reason a photo of the scene exists at all is because a member of the crew snapped a photograph of it. "We now have in the restoration, this scene showing the actual set-up that day. It is the only surviving photograph, and it is just a snapshot."

After seeing several minutes of still photos, Gitt states that people sometimes ask him which running time of *Lost Horizon* he prefers. The full 132-minute film, he claims, is important for academics and film enthusiasts, but Gitt prefers a more dynamic version.

> In terms of just entertainment for an audience, I kind of like an interim version, a version that includes all the action footage that we found in England and the French Canadian TV print, but maybe drop these still sections, but would include these speeches by the High Lama that Frank Capra wanted to leave in because those scenes are very static anyway, and the fact that there are a few still photographs or freeze frames, I don't think is very bothersome in that sequence. So, I think a running time of about 125 minutes, let's say, two hours and five minutes is sort of my personal favorite version, but ah, many people do seem to find the idea of seeing the original 132-minute version an attractive one and that's fine. I am glad we were able to do it and certainly to get the sound back, so you can hear what happened.

I have to agree with his penchant for a slightly shorter film. The scene that includes the snapshot taken by a crewmember is visually distracting and seems to do little for the film's continuity. The snapshot, of course, serves as indexical proof that the scene once existed, and Gitt recognizes the academic and archival desire for a film that is as complete as possible. But he is also cognizant of other audiences who prefer motion to stillness and can enjoy the film without visual identification of each scene that existed at its premiere in 1937.

While the 132-minute version of *Lost Horizon*, Gitt seems to suggest, can rest safely in the archive as the most original account of the film's premiere, a shorter version might be preferable, more enjoyable for general exhibition. Balancing the archival quest for completion and continuity with the film's function as entertainment, Gitt aims to recuperate the past as completely as possible while also considering the pleasures of present and future moviegoers. Gitt does not focus solely upon the past and its recovery; he is also engaged in figuring out how to situate the cinematic artifact in present-day culture.

Gitt explains (104 minutes into the film) that the scene the viewer is watching is a convention print for exhibitors and was never seen by general audiences. He points out that the sound does not synchronize between the lips and the voices because he used an alternate take that does not completely correspond with the soundtrack. He states that he edited it so "that it almost matches and works reasonably well. It should be in the film and it was the only way we could get it back in the film." As the scene changes, Champlin says to Gitt, "You become a filmmaker." Gitt replies, "Well, I don't want to become a filmmaker. The idea of restoring the film isn't to make changes to it. That isn't exactly making a change. It's trying to reconstruct it the best we can, but unfortunately in some cases we are missing material." "But you have to project yourself," Champlin responds, "into the filmmaker's mind, it seems to me." "Well, to a certain degree," Gitt replies. "You are just trying to put it back the way it was and when you are missing something and you find it, even though it isn't quite perfect, you use it."

Champlin's assertion that Gitt is a filmmaker is one Gitt refutes because he, of course, is not filmmaker but a film re-maker. Gitt explains that his role is to put the film back together, but when things are missing, he makes do with admittedly less-than-perfect solutions. Gitt's work on *Lost Horizon,* Champlin is suggesting, was a creative process that requires the knowledge and ingenuity of a filmmaker. But archival discourse does not usually acknowledge or much allow for the act of creativity in the restoration process. While Gitt dismisses the title of filmmaker outright, creativity's role in restoration is usually downplayed in such narratives. They typically privilege the rigor of the technological process instead. But at the same time, stories of restoration also detail the inventive ways that absences are overcome.

What remains of a film: its evidential images, written accounts, and what is left of its original celluloid and soundtrack, serve as a basis for making logical conclusions about how to offset the missing material. Historians regularly confront ambiguity and contradictory evidence because many of their sources of evidence do not survive. "And like all scientists who work outside of laboratories," Gaddis explains, "historians must use logic and imagination to overcome the resulting difficulties, their own equivalent of thought experiments, if you will."[13] Gaddis is not suggesting that historians are creators of fiction; rather he is proposing that historians use their imaginations while being simultaneously "tethered to and disciplined by sources."[14]

Similarly, the restorationist employs the methods of the historian to address what is missing from the film and the creativity of the filmmaker to compensate for its losses. While most restorationists feel more comfortable focusing on the logical processes of their work, they are also inventive film re-makers who use their knowledge of filmmaking as well as their imagination to offset cinematic absences. Restoration work, a logical and creative kind of history making, frames the cinematic past as an ongoing process of discovery that asks us to imagine and consider the many lives of a film.

As Gitt has noted throughout the *Lost Horizon* commentary, the work of the restorationist is neither always complete nor successful. After twenty-five years of effort, Capra's film, Gitt explains in detail, is still not faultless. Gitt's focus on the gaps and what remains unknowable suggests *Lost Horizon's* history is not yet finalized. The imperfect restoration makes the cinematic past legible, but its disruptions remind us that this imperfect art/science cannot entirely recover a cinematic past. Some cinematic losses brought on by disregard and the passing of time, the gaps suggest, simply cannot be known. While Gitt many not be entirely satisfied with the seven minutes of frozen images in the restored *Lost Horizon,* they are important, for they help to tell the story of the film's past.

Interrupting the flow of the film's narrative, the gaps startle audiences into remembering that they are viewing an incomplete interpretation of cinematic history. Seven minutes of stillness in *Lost Horizon* reminds us that new representations and alternative meanings of history are still possible. Because present-day restoration discourse resists singularity and finitude, it inevitably encourages engagement in an ongoing and open relationship with the cinematic past. Like Iris Barry and her contemporaries, Gitt and his fellow restorationists and archivists, are helping to shape how contemporary people view films and make sense of cinema history.

In *Lost Horizon,* the High Lama (Sam Jaffe) bequeaths his leadership role onto Bob Conway (Ronald Colman). But he also speaks to the ways in which modern people transform and domesticate the past, and his claims about history making inadvertently describe contemporary practices of film restoration. "You my son, will live through the storm," says the High Lama.

> You will preserve the fragrance of our history and add to it a touch of your own mind. Beyond that my vision weakens. But I see in the great distance, a new world stirring in the ruins, clumsily but in hopefulness—seeking its lost but legendary treasures, and they will all be here my son, hidden behind the mountains, in the Valley of the Blue Moon. Preserved as by a miracle.

These words of the High Lama are a fitting conclusion and a reminder that when we go about restoring the cinematic image, we are preserving the fragrance of the past for our own understanding, enjoyment, and even comfort. Each generation's principles and practices of history making are powerful reassurances that the gap between the past and the present has the potential to be lessened.

CONCLUSION

As you read this, there are thousands of films pouring into our archives, while thousands more are disintegrating or are simply missing. A handful of archivists are confidently piecing together filmic fragments while a few others are fretting over incomprehensible cinematic remains. Catalogers are busy doing authority work, but are anxious about all of the films they have been ignoring. A scholar "discovers" a film, a researcher requests to see a classic, and an archivist steps into a vault, peering at the films that will likely never be viewed again. In the archive, at this moment, the filmic past is being pieced together, revered, ignored, or forgotten all together.

Film collectors and archivists over the past eighty years have constructed a spectacular visual map of the twentieth century, and in the process of gathering together and caring for the fragments of the cinematic past, they have unintentionally fashioned a history of the United States that perhaps surpasses the Benjaminian historiographic ideal. Attempting to radically reshape the way history was constructed so to resist historicism, Walter Benjamin gave voice to what had been silenced and attempted to bring the past closer to those confronting it. Rather than a cumulative narrative in which time flows smoothly from past to future, Benjamin's nineteenth-century Paris is a paratactic history where any moment has the potential to conjoin with any other moment. Benjamin juxtaposed the ephemeral and the anecdotal, scattering it about, in hopes that his readers might conjure up flashes of insight. Often preferring to allow the words he collected speak for themselves without (or with very little) authorial translation and interpretation, Benjamin's work as a historian sometimes resembles the labor of the archivist—collecting, rearranging, and offering up the remnants of the past. Showing rather than telling, exhibiting rather than explaining, Benjamin cajoled his readers to break free from the dream world of history and come closer to the past.

The film archiving project at the beginning of the twenty-first century works similarly—to enter the archive is to intermingle with ghosts that largely have been left to their own devices. With its hundreds of thousands of hours of moving images, the contemporary film archive gives movement to the last hundred years, invoking a Borges-like map—with all of the twentieth century's palaces, alleyways, villages, and dark corners. Archival wanderers can suture together a number of idiosyncratic histories of the past century by accessing its spectacles and then weaving their way through the established routes, unexplained pathways, and dead ends of the filmic ruins of the last century.

What began as purposeful and disciplined collecting in the first half of the twentieth century ultimately drifted into a monstrous and scattered custodial project during the last decades. Collector-archivists during the 1930s and 1940s had a far more decisive mission than the custodian-archivists of today, for they imagined that they could collect particular kinds of films so to tell specific stories about the United States. And for the most part, their plan to soothe cultural anxieties by amassing films worked quite well; they systematically collected and created a visual mythology of the country's cinematic, artistic, political, and moral prowess. Early film collections, at the Museum of Modern Art, the Library of Congress, and the National Archives, were viewed as jewels that could infuse their real and (more often than not) theoretical audiences with pride and patriotism.

While the intentions of early collectors and proponents of national film collections varied, all were motivated in part by a desire to collect images that could persuade, inform, educate, and inspire in the years before the domestication of moving images. The belief that there could be some control over film collections' meanings was reasonable enough during the decades before moving images became ubiquitous. Before the advent of televisions, VCRs, DVD players, computers, and the rest, it was fairly easy to construct a moving image fiefdom, for there were far fewer accessible moving images with competing messages, and the public did not yet expect that nearly any film produced should be made available to them almost instantaneously by way of their personal screens. Stern believers in the rhetorical power of film, Iris Barry, Archibald MacLeish, Will Hays, and their peers sought to control cinema's early history in the years when the United States was emerging as the global giant. Their filmic fortresses resembled the optimism of a high school history book that contained powerful visual evidence as to why the nation deserved its escalating identity as a cultural and political world power.

But such control over the archive's meanings did not last. The development of the American Film Institute during the Cold War marked the final chapter of the nationalistic impulses of the archive's first wave. So to remain internationally competitive, the developers of the AFI pushed for a broad and brand new kind of archival access, so up-and-coming filmmakers could study revered industry films. Cracking open the doors to the second wave of the film archive, the AFI helped to shift the archive away from an ethos of secrecy to a culture that placed value on accessibility. Concurrently, technological advances, such as the VCR, cable television, and the personal computer created new viewing platforms that enabled people to watch classic films outside of a repertoire theater. Rather quickly, the public grew accustomed to and hungry for regular and convenient access to older films.

With the new widespread interest and public demand for classic films, the country's film archives were pushed into the national spotlight. Their time had come; the archival door was blown wide open, and the second wave of archivists marched in. When the bright light poured into the archive in the 1980s and early 1990s, second-generation archivists discovered an enormous amount of disintegrating, unidentified films stacked high in the archive. At the same time, public expectations and demand for archival access grew, making it increasingly difficult to maintain a command over collections and control over archival meanings. And all the while, the films kept pouring in.

The death knell of historicism sounded when Congress enacted a law to protect the nation's filmic memories. Such a law, of course, was a symptom that it was no longer really possible to protect or contain the meanings within the archive. With the signing of the first National Film Preservation Act and the creation of the National Film Registry, the archival film was finally a privileged national artifact, but simultaneously it brought to the fore the fact that the national film record was mostly built upon absences. Twenty-five films placed on the registry each year was certainly a nod to the civilizing of our cinematic heritage, but it simultaneously called attention to the thousands upon thousands of orphans that were still running wild.

After two public hearings and the creation of a national report, the federal government put its money on the orphans and urged film studios to step up and start caring for their own films. Small films made by nonindustry filmmakers began receiving almost as much archival attention as the Hollywood stories that had reigned supreme for more than fifty years, resulting in a certain flattening of the archival hierarchy. By the end of the twentieth century, the archive was no longer a place where only industry films, big name filmmakers, and Hollywood dreams were privileged. Researchers desiring to compose their histories by way of the film archive had, at last, multifarious routes from which to choose. And all the while, films continued to flow into the archive.

As we stand in the foothills of the digital future and look behind us, it is clear that during the twentieth century, film and its preservation was imagined and systemized only as analog: celluloid in film cans. But the analog world is giving way to a digital one, and as a result, the moving image archive will change dramatically, perhaps more than it ever has in its brief history. Archivists know there is much to do to prepare for the archive's dramatic transition from analog to digital. More and more films come to the archive as a code of zeroes and ones instead of in cans, and with increasing expectations and demands for cultural collections to be digitally accessible, the moving image archive will necessarily make the digital transition. Like the analog archive, the digital archive faces complicated issues of storage and access, but the strategies to overcome problems with storage space, technological obsolescence, and accessibility in a digital archive remain inexact. While digital archiving is a complex, expensive, and challenging endeavor, many archivists believe it has the potential to positively and dramatically alter the relationship that educators, researchers, and the public have with archival moving images. Visionaries and proponents of the digital archive believe digitization will greatly enhance moving image accessibility.

While archivists dreaming in the digital must focus on the challenges of digital collection, storage, and preservation, they stress the liberating potential of its accessibility. The analog archive often requires researchers to be physically present in a moving image archive so to see materials, and unless researchers know exactly what they were looking for, it is also necessary to be at the archive to comprehend and distinguish between collections and to understand an archive's underlying logic. The dramatic success of Rick Prelinger's Internet Archive suggests that researchers, educators, and the public are hungry for access to digitized archival moving images. While institutional archives are barely creeping toward their digitization goals, the Internet Archive is the prototype for the moving-image archive in the digital age. The moving images along with the archive's texts, audio, archived web pages, and software are particularly convenient and easy to access. Often I use the Internet Archive while teaching, using digitized moving images to visually enhance ideas that arise during classroom discussions. Access to moving images on the site is instantaneous, and my students and I can use the moving images immediately and spontaneously to reinforce my professorial objectives as well as broaden classroom conversations.

To be sure, the Internet Archive, which was born digital, has expanded the vision and exploded the boundaries of archival accessibility; however, at present, among traditional moving image archives, it still stands alone, for analog archives confront significant challenges as they begin their digital reorientation. In July 2007, the Digital Library Federation (DLF) hosted a seminar on moving image digitization. Organized by Prelinger and Peter Brantley of DLF, a group of moving-image experts discussed how to "facilitate broader access to the incredible trove of film, and video held in archives, libraries, museums, broadcast stations, and other sources."[1] The group, named Lot 49, believes that access should be the primary goal of the contemporary moving image archive. Without it, they reason, government, donations, and grant funding for archives will continue to dwindle. Lot 49 agreed to conduct an assessment of the present state of the moving image archive and help develop a set of principles to lead to increased digitization and access to collections.

The assessment was compiled in part by a five-month survey of seventy archives that house moving image collections (ranging in size from

200 to 112,000 items). The goal of the survey was to determine the "nature and condition" of the archives' collections and to what extent digitization had been integrated into the archive. The results strongly suggest that archives are understaffed and underfunded, and they are too overwhelmed by caring for their analog collections to focus on digitization.[2] Cataloging backlogs, outdated records and technology, the disappearance of institutional memory as senior archivists retire, complicated rights issues, and insufficient staffing, viewing copies, computers, physical and server space confound large and small moving image archives. Analog nightmares, in other words, now drown out digital dreams.

As archivists creep toward their digitization goals, they face, among others, two significant challenges. One is the continual evolution of technology. Moving image archives technologies will necessarily adapt to digital technologies to perform archival enterprises; simultaneously, archives will maintain their analog collections and technologies. Archives will be faced with trying to contain and preserve both their analog and digital material and the systems that enable materials to be accessed in the future. Digitization creates both an information explosion and an increased threat of information extinction. Archivists, for example, will need to continue to develop, maintain, and preserve traditional metadata, such as intellectual and physical descriptions, but they will also have to preserve the media on which digital data is stored, the hardware needed to play it, and the applications that use it.

No current or presently imaginable digital system is as reliable as 35 mm film. It is "the shining example of a standardized and sustainable format that is widely adopted, globally interoperable, stable, and well understood. The bottom line is that any system proposing to replace photochemical film technology must meet or exceed film's capabilities."[3] The switch to digital does not guarantee long-term access to moving image and sound content, for technical threats such as data corruptions and hardware and software systems obsolescence and the threat of human error pose a major risk to digital archive assets. To be sure, in order for the transition from analog to digital to be successful, there must be well-considered, cautious, collaborative, and standardized plans.

Cost is the other substantial challenge facing the archival transition from analog to digital. The efforts to shift to digital technologies will incur great costs to archives that do much of their work by way of grants, government funding, and donations. "Virtually all the archives said they received grants, held fund-raisers, or received private donations in order to support projects," the Lot 49 report explained, "but very few of these projects were digitization projects. Most of the money funds collection stabilization and development, including new cataloging projects and transfers of obsolete film and video formats for preservation and access."[4] Because archives must scramble to fund and care for their analog systems, there is little time and only modest funds for digitization. The annual cost of preserving film archival master material is $1,059 per title. But to preserve the same material digitally costs $12,514 per year.[5] The dramatic difference in cost between analog and digital lies in the "higher levels of investment to support the ongoing digital preservation process which many include digital migration."[6]

Facing enormous costs, archives will necessarily have to make choices about which materials to save and make digitally accessible. "The save everything" philosophy of the analog archive is not economically feasible in the digital age. Studios are producing so much digital content that some of it must be discarded. The exorbitant costs of digital systems have obvious consequences for an archival culture invested in saving everything and making it accessible. While archivists have been reluctant to dismiss any moving image material as irrelevant, in the digital archive, at least in the decades to come, choices will necessarily be made. While studios will discard what they consider to be irrelevant digital material, archives, in the foreseeable future, will focus their efforts on digitizing their most popular and well-known titles. Analog material that has not been digitized will become increasingly invisible to users accustomed to accessing moving image content by way of the digital domain. The contemporary moving image archival desire is that all people may have convenient access to a wide array of moving images. Surely, such sites as the Internet Archive and the Library of Congress's American Memory provide us with an inkling of what we might look forward to in the digital domain. Yet, there are still many challenges to overcome. Archives that are currently overwhelmed by their analog systems must now dramatically increase their efforts and operating costs so as to transition to the digital domain.

We will likely bury parts of our cinematic heritage under analog and digital piles, perhaps to be rediscovered later, perhaps not. The digital transition will surely result in a dramatic increase in the amount of people accessing, watching, and integrating archival moving images into their lives, though they will be watching only a diminutive proportion of the moving images stored and cared for in vaults and hard drives in archives around the country. While contemporary archival culture embraces a wide range of moving image genres—amateur films, industrial films, and pornography included, archivists in the near digital future will have to make difficult choices about which materials to make digitally accessible. In their choosing of which histories to make visible, digital archivists, like their analog counterparts before them, will shape how and what we understand of our filmic and cultural pasts.

The digital archive, like its predecessor, will work to collect the filmic and cultural meanings of the last and current century. But it will not be easy. The moving image archive is an unruly place that is difficult and expensive to control. Filmic images infiltrate our archives in massive numbers and then threaten to disappear—hiding beneath multitudes of other ephemeral worlds. The logic of the archive is driven by replication. Because the film archive staves off the impermanence of the past by collecting mountains of impermanent objects and codes, the archive can only survive by duplicating itself over and over again.

At the beginning of the twenty-first century, archivists work professionally and diligently to contain their collections, but the sheer amount of materials make containment nearly impossible. Today's curious researchers who access the film archive have the potential to have a far more adventurous and liberating archival experience than their predecessors. The massive amounts of material, the collections that represent nearly every facet of the twentieth-century experience, and scanty documentation create practically perfect conditions for those bold researchers who desire to build their own corridors through the past. Certainly, there are practical problems. Too much material with too few guideposts can make archival wandering frustrating. But the frontier conditions of the contemporary film archive may quite possibly represent the future of history making, and if we stop resisting its somewhat chaotic nature, we might begin to better understand its capacity to reshape the way we make sense of the past. Put another way, to accept that the film archive does not resemble or function like any other sanctioned storehouse of memory, we have a better chance of understanding how the film archive can better foster innovative methods of accessing and narrating the past.

We need only look to the work of restorationists to see that the re-visioning of history is not only possible but is already taking place within the archive. While restorationists do privilege a film's originary status, they are not, nor should they be tethered to it. The restorationist asks us to consider all of a film's past lives: its theatrical premiere, subsequent modifications, its fall into obscurity, its neglect, as well as its resurrection. The restored film suggests that our knowledge, even about the recent past, is never complete, and future amendments to our historical understanding are more likely if our methods for piecing together the past remain transparent. The restored film is not simply a stodgy signifier of the past; rather it is a unique cinematic form that brings the past up close to us and then pulls it away. Its capacity to juxtapose the continuous with the discontinuous offers us the potential for new insights about our relationship with history, for at the moment when the past and present collide, there is, as Benjamin believed, the possibility for illumination.

And yet we have not yet begun to fully exploit the resources within the archive. Many may grumble that the archive in the United States is still too complicated to access, pointing to other time traveling portals that are much easier to use. Is it possible that YouTube is all that we need? YouTube users skim along the surface of moving image history without caution. A technology that requires little commitment from us, it acknowledges that sometimes history is just easy come, easy go. The archive, on the other hand, suggests that history is hard work. It requires us to collect the refuse of the past, mend it, replicate it, and guard it, all the while implying that the past is nearly impossible to mend, to replicate, and to guard. YouTube represents our ironic, playful stance toward history, while the archive signifies our diligent, puritanical approach to bridging the past with the present. Taken together, they offer us a compelling portrait of how contemporary people view history: with both reverence and impudence. It is a dialectic that ensures that the past, at least for now, will neither vanish because of our carelessness nor be imprisoned due to our veneration.

NOTES

Introduction

1. A master positive print is generated from the camera negative for the purpose of creating additional duplicate negatives. Viewing prints are made for circulation, allowing the original film and/or the master prints to remain within the archive.

2. A dupe negative is a negative element printed from a positive print.

3. Mulvey, *Death 24x a Second*, 52.

4. Charney and Schwartz, introduction to *Cinema and the Invention of Modern Life*, 10.

5. Hansen, "America, Paris, the Alps," 365–66.

6. Ibid., 377.

7. Benjamin, "The Work of Art in the Age of Mechanical Reproduction," in *Illuminations*, 236.

8. Kracauer, *Theory of Film*, 165.

9. Cummings, *Making Blood White*, 4.

10. Rosen, introduction to *boundary 2*, 6.

11. Schwartz, "Walter Benjamin for Historians," 1740.

12. Benjamin, "On the Concept of History" (1940), in *Selected Writings*, edited by Eiland and Jennings, 4: 462nn2a, 3.

13. Buck-Morss, *The Dialectics of Seeing*, 218.

14. Eiland, "Reception in Distraction," 63.

15. Schwartz, "Walter Benjamin for Historians," 1741.

16. Derrida, *Archive Fever*, 4.

17. Ibid., 11.

18. Manoff, "Theories of the Archives," 12.

19. Ibid.

20. Bloch, *The Historian's Craft.*

21. Foucault, *Discipline and Punish* (1977); *Madness and Civilization* (1988); *The Order of Things* (1974).

22. Dirks, "The Crimes of Colonialism," 175

23. See Bennett, *Pasts Beyond Memory*; Wagoner, "Precolonial Intellectuals and the Production of Colonial Knowledge," 783–814; Stoler, "Colonial Archives and the Arts of Governance," 87–109; Mathur, "History and Anthropology in South Asia," 89–106.

24. See Aguirre, *Informal Empire*; Lindquist, "'The Mightiest Instrument of the Physical Discoverer': The Visual 'Imagination' and the Victorian Observer," 171–99; Blouin, "History and Memory," 296–98.

25. Levine, "Discipline and Pleasure," 324.

26. Brown and Davis-Brown, "The Making of Memory," 22.

27. Voss and Werner, "Toward a Poetics of the Archive," ii.

28. Greetham, "'Who's In, Who's Out,'" 10.

29. Ibid.

30. Ibid., 19.

31. Lynch, "Archives in Formation," 83.

32. I did ethnographic research at UCLA, the Museum of Modern Art, the Library of Congress, Northeast Historic Film, the Smithsonian's Human Studies Film Archives, and the National Archives' division of Motion Picture Films and Sound and Video Recordings. I took tours of the facilities and conducted forty hours of formal interviews with archivists. I have attended annual Association of Moving Image Archivists (AMIA) conferences and have been a member of the AMIA LISTSERV for six years. I also attend, make presentations, and co-organize the Northeast Historic Film summer symposium each year, a meeting where scholars, archivists, and researchers deliberate issues concerning the moving image archive and collections. I serve as an advisor to NHF and spent one summer occasionally volunteering as a cataloger there. I was the chair of the Media Archives Committee for the Society of Cinema and Media Studies for two years. And I work with Karen Underhill, the Special Collections director at Northern Arizona University, and Jonathan Pringle, an archivist at the Museum of Northern Arizona, to determine what significant moving images are in their collections and how to make them more accessible to researchers and the public. These endeavors, as well as the hundreds of hours more of face to face and e-mail conversations I have had with archivists from

around the country, have helped me to understand and analyze the current culture of the moving image archive.

33. Gracy, "Documenting Communities of Practice," 337.

Chapter 1. What to Show the World

1. National Film Preservation Foundation, "Why Save Film?," http://www.filmpreservation.org.

2. Barry, "The Film Library and How it Grew," 22.

3. Slide, *Nitrate Won't Wait*, 18.

4. May, *Screening Out the Past*, 179.

5. The MPPDA was not the only industry organization in the 1920s that sought to help soothe internal and external industry relations and enhance Hollywood's reputation and ultimately determine that film collecting would benefit the industry and the organization. The Academy of Motion Picture Arts and Sciences (AMPAS) founded in 1927 was organized for the purpose of protecting the welfare of members, mediating labor disputes, and bettering the industry's reputation; however, those objectives were mostly put aside by the end of the 1930s. Today, of course, the Academy is best known for its annual award ceremony, an idea originally initiated by Douglas Fairbanks, Sr., the first president of the Academy. As one of his final acts as president, he initiated a plan for the Academy to bestow awards of merit for distinctive achievement (the first ceremony was held in 1929).

AMPAS also has a history of contributing to educational pursuits so to benefit its members and help advance the film industry, which included collecting materials relevant to the Academy's interests. Its earliest library in the late 1920s was composed of various motion picture magazines and technical references for studio employees enrolled in the Academy's School in Fundamentals of Sound Recording and Reproduction. By the 1940s, the Academy library rivaled both the Museum of Modern Art and the Library of Congress as having one of the most complete collections of motion picture materials in the world. The Academy's library included motion picture scripts from the most important films since 1925, books, statistical and historical data, domestic and foreign trade magazines, still photographs from the one thousand most important films since 1915, and a file of production information that included data from nearly twenty thousand films that had been produced since 1900.

The library did not focus its collecting pursuits on motion pictures; however, in 1943, the library did construct a special collection of 275 war films, specifically films produced in the United States, England, Canada, Russia, and Mexico. Similar to the wartime collaboration between the Library of Congress and the Museum of Modern Art, which will be discussed in the pages to come, the library's initial film collecting occurred as a result of AMPAS's desire to help the war effort. However, by the end of World War II, AMPAS did begin adding older films to its holdings. By 1946, the library had ninety-five reels of old silent films. Eventually, a separate Academy Film Archive assumed responsibility for the Academy's film collections. The Academy Film Archive currently holds more than twelve thousand items. A large part of the present-day collection is behind-the-scenes films, which include films about filmmaking, Academy Award broadcasts, and home movies of directors and producers.

6. Slide, *Nitrate Won't Wait,* 26.

7. "Hays Asks Coolidge for Film Archives," *New York Times,* September 1, 1926.

8. Ibid.

9. Ibid.

10. "Historical Film Subjects Suggested for Government Vaults," *New York Times,* September 12, 1926.

11. "Films Put on Ice for Fans Yet Unborn," *New York Times,* October 24, 1926.

12. Rosen, *Change Mummified,* 29.

13. "History and Motion Pictures," 1.

14. "Can Films be Preserved?" 521.

15. Ciarlante, "The Origin of Motion Picture and Sound Recording Collection Policy in the National Archives," 2.

16. Ibid., 22.

17. R.D.W. Connor, "New Archives to Shelter Movies and Many Records," *New York Times,* February 10, 1935.

18. Once motion pictures were protected by copyright laws and paper prints were no longer deposited, the library had no way to maintain copies of motion pictures that came to the library for copyright registration. From 1912 to 1942, the library sent motion pictures back to their producers within one day of their receipt, accepting only materials such as scripts, posters, or credit sheets for copyright deposit. One of the ways in which MacLeish worked to build a national collection was to restore the original conditions of the motion picture copyright deposit.

19. Goodrum, *The Library of Congress,* 22.

20. Herrick, "Toward a National Film Collection," 6.

21. Ibid., 9.

22. Grimm, "A Paper Print Pre-history," 207.

23. MacLeish, *Annual Report of the Librarian of Congress, 1942,* 20.

24. Walls, "Motion Picture Incunabula in the Library of Congress," 158.

25. "Lost Films of Yesteryear," editorial, New York Times, May 7, 1943.

26. Howard Walls, *New York Times,* May 20, 1943, 20.

27. "Congress Library Drops Motion Picture Project," *New York Times,* August 22, 1947.

28. Walls, "Motion Picture Incunabula in the Library of Congress," 156.

29. Haidee Wasson's wonderful book *Museum Movies: The Museum of Modern Art and the Birth of Art Cinema* fully chronicles and analyzes the impact Iris Barry and the MoMA Film Library had on film culture.

30. Wasson, *Museum Movies,* 87.

31. Ibid.

32. Barry, "The Museum of Modern Art Film Library," 14.

33. Ibid.

34. Barry, "The Museum of Modern Art Film Library Last Year and This," 41.

35. Wasson, "'Some Kind of Racket,'" 24.

36. Barry, "The Film Library and How it Grew," 23.

37. Wasson, "'Some Kind of Racket,'" 20.

38. Barry, "The Museum of Modern Art Film Library," 16.

39. Ibid.

40. Barry, "Why Wait for Prosperity?" 136.

41. Ibid., 137.

42. Barry, "Films for History," 258.

43. Barry, "Motion Pictures as a Field for Research," 208.

44. Barry influenced, shaped, practiced, and modeled film scholarship for a generation of film scholars, and her work has had a lasting impact on film history. In 1939, D. W. Griffith donated his papers, negatives, and prints to the museum. By collecting, exhibiting, highlighting, and writing about Griffith's work, Barry was a major influence in the construction of D. W. Griffith's position in the American film canon. If his films had not survived, if Griffith—an artist living in semiobscurity in the late thirties—had not donated his papers, prints, and negatives to the museum, and if Barry had not believed his work to be important, it is likely that his films and his position as an early film director would not play as an important role in the current interpretation of American film history. At the time that Griffith donated his materials to the Film Library, his films and his career were not well regarded because those who considered his works at all focused on his films' content.

Through the study of his films' composition, Barry defined Griffith's work in a new way; he was an artistic pioneer who had laid down all of the basic artistic principles of film. She highlighted the innovative techniques that Griffith created in her book about his films and career, noting his development of crosscutting, close-ups, long shots, tracking shots, and camera angles, some of which had been attributed to German filmmakers years after Griffith used them in his films. Students of art and culture did not immediately accept Barry's proclamation, but by the time Barry's book was reissued in 1965, Griffith's work was generally accepted as a critical chapter in the art of film and its history.

Barry's observations and study of Griffith's films changed how film history imagined his work, but more important her work was constructed so to demonstrate that film was art, and its scholarly examination requires that it be examined firsthand and not from memory. She established that a film should be studied as an individual entity and in comparison to other film works. This method of film scholarship helped to justify the necessity for the Film Library's film collection and the preservation and exhibition of the films Barry had helped to obtain.

45. Hart, "Making Democracy Safe for the World," 55.

46. Ibid., 81.

47. Koppes and Black, "What to Show the World," 98.

48. Ibid., 103–4.

49. MacLeish, *Annual Report of the Librarian of Congress, 1942*, 20.

50. Deming, "The Library of Congress Film Project," 12.

51. Ibid., 31–32.

52. Quoted in Spehr, "It Was Fifty Years Ago This Month," 175.

53. Decherney, *Hollywood and the Culture Elite*, 156.

54. Deming, "The Library of Congress Film Project," 5.

55. Under the aegis of the Library of Congress, the National Film Preservation Board, the National Film Registry, and the National Film Preservation Foundation are present-day institutional efforts that help to maintain a national archival identity. The NFPB, established by the National Film Preservation Act in 1988, is responsible for choosing the films for the NFR (besides the bit of press the films receive at the time they are added to the registry, they are eventually preserved under the direction of the Library of Congress). From 1989 to 2009, 525 films have been added to the registry. The films chosen to the registry reflect the various interests of archives across the United States. Hollywood films are well represented, but orphan, amateur, independent, and experimental films, as well as documentaries, short subjects, and music videos are also on the registry.

Not a national film collection, the registry effectively promotes archival interests and speaks to the significance of the country's cinematic heritage. The National Film Preservation Foundation, affiliated with the National Film Preservation Board, has since 1997, operated primarily as a grant program giving money to institutions for the preservation of films that would likely not be preserved without public support. While the public is likely more interested and familiar with the National Film Registry, archivists view the NFPF as incredibly important to the health of their collections, for it grants preservation funding for orphan films and many small non-Hollywood films.

Chapter 2. Accessibility, Authenticity, and Anxiety

1. Young, "An American Film Institute: A Proposal," 38.

2. Ibid., 41.

3. Ibid., 42.

4. Ibid., 40.

5. Ibid., 45.

6. Ibid., 46.

7. Ibid., 50.

8. Horne, "Experiments in Propaganda," 191.

9. Horne's essay, "Experiments in Propaganda" details Stevens's contributions to the USIA Motion Picture Division and also speaks to the filmmaker James Blue who worked under Stevens.

10. Tilton, Martin, Jr., and Green, *Organization and Location of the American Film Institute*, 10.

11. Ibid., 80.

12. Ibid., 14.

13. The relationships between private collectors and the archive are certainly significant to archival history, but the collaborations between collectors and archives were essentially done in secret—creating a historical black hole. Slide's chapter about collectors is helpful, but even the wisest archivists I could track down, shrugged their shoulders and told me that it is an invisible history.

14. Slide, *Nitrate Won't Wait*, 45.

15. Tilton, Martin, Jr., and Green, *Organization and Location of the American Film Institute*, 97.

16. It is not entirely clear why 16 mm was not an option for the Stanford authors. The circulation of 16 mm films had been going on for decades.

17. Tilton, Martin, Jr., and Green, *Organization and Location of the American Film Institute*, 87.

18. Ibid., 93.

19. Ibid., 96.

20. Kula, "Introduction: Moving Image/American Image," 10.

21. Mann, "The Evolution of American Moving Image Preservation," 1.

22. Callenbach, "The Unloved One," 42–54.

23. Kula, "Introduction: Moving Image/American Image," 13.

24. Peck, foreword to *The American Film Heritage*, 5.

25. Kula, "Introduction: Moving Image/American Image," 13.

26. Mann, "The Evolution of American Moving Image Preservation," 9.

27. Slide, *Nitrate Won't Wait*, 87.

28. Naremore, "Authorship," 13–14.

29. Ray, *How a Film Theory Got Lost*, 11.

30. Gary Burns, "Colorization," http://archives.museum.tv/.

31. Vincent Canby, "'Colorization' Defaces Black and White Film Classics," *New York Times*, November 2, 1986.

32. Dempsey, "Colorization," 2.

33. Richard E. Mooney, "Tainted, Tinted Movies," *New York Times*, November 16, 1986.

34. Quoted in Aljean Harmetz, "Huston Protests Coloring of 'Falcon,'" *New York Times*, November 14, 1986.

35. Art Shifrin, "On Coloring Films," *New York Times*, December 21, 1986.

36. Quoted in Harmetz, "Huston Protests Coloring of 'Falcon.'"

37. Woody Allen, "The Colorization of Films Insults Artists and Society," *New York Times*, June 28, 1987.

38. Ibid.

39. Quoted in Dowd, "Film Stars Protest Coloring," *New York Times*, May 13, 1987.

40. Grainge, *Monochrome Memories*, 162.

41. Ibid., 162–63.

42. Quoted in Andrew Yarrow, "Action but No Consensus on Film Coloring," *New York Times*, July 11, 1988.

43. Ibid.

44. Ibid.

45. Slide, *Nitrate Won't Wait*, 131.

46. McGreevey and Yeck, *Our Movie Heritage*, 34.

47. Ibid., 165.

48. Van Camp, "Colorization Revisited," 450.

49. Beck, "Inglorious Color," 12.

50. Grainge, *Monochrome Memories*, 170.

Chapter 3. Film Preservation 1993

1. Melville and Simmon, *Film Preservation 1993*, 1: 1.

2. Ibid., 1: ix.

3. Ibid., 1: 5.

4. Ibid., 1: 3.

5. Jensen, "The Culture Wars," 20.

6. Ibid., 18.

7. Melville and Simmon, *Film Preservation 1993*, 3: 78–79.

8. Ibid., 2: 15.

9. Ibid., 3: 81.

10. Ibid., 3: 50–51.

11. Ibid., 2: 4.

12. Ibid., 1: 58.

13. Ibid., 1: 60.

14. Ibid., 1: 5.
15. Ibid., 2: 15.
16. Ibid., 2: 9.
17. Ibid., 3: 12.
18. Ibid., 3: 17.
19. Ibid., 3: 19.
20. Ibid.
21. Ibid.
22. Ibid., 3: 72–73.
23. Ibid., 3: 29.
24. Ibid.
25. Ibid., 3: 84.
26. Ibid.
27. Ibid., 3: 41.
28. Ibid.
29. Ibid.
30. Ibid., 3: 45.
31. Ibid., 3: 49.
32. Ibid., 3: 45.
33. Ibid., 3: 51.
34. Ibid.
35. Ibid., 3: 127.
36. Ibid., 3: 129.

Chapter 4. The Archive at the End of the Century

1. Horak, "Film History and Film Preservation" *Screening the Past*, 1.
2. Robert Rosen, "A Retrospective Look," http://www.cinema.ucla.edu/PR/rosen.html.
3. Geary, *Phantoms of Remembrance*, 10.
4. James Billington, "Welcome Message from the Librarian of Congress," http://www.loc.gov/about/.
5. Billington, "Facts at a Glance," http://www.loc.gov/about/reports/annualreports/fy2009.
6. Nora, *Realms of Memory*, 1.
7. Gaddis, *The Landscape of History*, 136.
8. Ibid.
9. Ibid., 141.
10. Nora, *Realms of Memory*, 3.
11. Benjamin, *The Arcades*, 211.

Chapter 5. Film Restoration

1. Lowenthal, *The Past Is a Foreign Country,* 412.

2. Bowser, "Some Principles of Film Restoration," 172.

3. Ibid.

4. Usai, *The Death of Cinema,* 39.

5. Bowser, "Some Principles of Film Restoration," 172.

6. Zizek, *Looking Awry,* 114.

7. I requested an interview with Packard, but he did not respond to my request.

8. Brandi, "Theory of Restoration, II," 339.

9. David Francis, "Motion Picture Conservation at the Library of Congress," http://loc.gov/rr/mopic/mppresdf.html.

10. Wostry, "Sodom and Gomorrah: Notes on a Reconstruction," 38.

11. Bowser, "Some Principles of Film Restoration," 173.

12. Gaddis, *The Landscape of History,* 135.

13. Ibid., 43

14. Ibid.

Conclusion

1. Mohan, *Environmental Scan of Moving Image Collections in the United States,* Digital Library Federation, 2008, 2, http://www.scribd.com/doc/5347688/Lot49.

2. Ibid., 16.

3. Ibid., 56.

4. Ibid., 16.

5. Davis, *Digital Dilemma: Strategic Issues in Archiving and Accessing Digital Motion Picture Materials,* Academy of Motion Picture Arts and Sciences, 2007, 2, http://www.oscars.org/science-technology/council/projects/digitaldilemma/.

6. Ibid., 45.

BIBLIOGRAPHY

Aguirre, Robert. *Informal Empire: Mexico and Central America in Victorian Culture*. Minneapolis: University of Minnesota Press, 2005.

Barry, Iris. "The Film Library and How it Grew." *Film Quarterly* 22 (1969): 19–27.

———. "Films for History." *Special Libraries* 30 (1939): 258–60.

———. "Motion Pictures as a Field for Research." *College Art Journal* 4 (1945): 206–9.

———. "The Museum of Modern Art Film Library." *Sight and Sound* 5 (1936): 14–16.

———. "The Museum of Modern Art Film Library Last Year and This." *Magazine of Art* 30 (1937): 40–44.

———. "Why Wait for Prosperity?" *Hollywood Quarterly* 1 (1946): 131–37.

Beck, Bernard. "Inglorious Color." *Society* 24 (1987): 4–12.

Benjamin, Walter. *The Arcades Project.* Translated by Howard Eiland and Kevin McLaughlin. Cambridge, Mass.: Harvard University Press, 1999.

———. *Illuminations.* Edited by Hannah Arendt. Translated by Harry Zohn. New York: Schocken Books, 1969.

———. "On the Concept of History" (1940). In *Selected Writings,* edited by Howard Eiland and Michael W. Jennings. Translated by Edmund Jephcott et al. Cambridge, Mass.: Harvard University Press, 2003.

Bennett, Tony. *Pasts Beyond Memory, Evolution, Museums, Colonialism.* London: Routledge, 2004.

Bloch, Marc. *The Historian's Craft.* Manchester, U.K.: Manchester University Press, 1954.

Blouin, Francis. "History and Memory: The Problem of the Archive." *PMLA* 119 (2004): 296–98.

Bowser, Eileen. "Some Principles of Film Restoration." *Griffithiana* 38/39 (1990): 172–73.

Brandi, Cesare. "Theory of Restoration, II." In *Historical and Philosophical Issues in the Conservation of Cultural Heritage,* edited by Nicholas Price, Mansfield Talley, and Alessandra Vaccaro. Los Angeles: Getty Conservation Institute, 1996.

Brown, Richard Harvey, and Beth Davis-Brown. "The Making of Memory: The Politics of Archives, Libraries, and Museums in the Construction of National Consciousness." *History of the Human Sciences* 11 (1998): 17–32.

Buck-Morss, Susan. *The Dialectics of Seeing: Walter Benjamin and "The Arcades Project."* Cambridge, Mass.: MIT Press, 1991.

Callenbach, Ernest. "The Unloved One: Crisis at the American Film Institute." *Film Quarterly* 24 (1971): 42–54.

"Can Films be Preserved for Posterity?" *Motography* 13 (April 3, 1915): 521.

Charney, Leo, and Vanessa Schwartz, eds. *Cinema and the Invention of Modern Life*. Berkeley: University of California Press, 1995.

Ciarlante, Marjorie H. "The Origin of Motion Picture and Sound Recording Collection Policy in the National Archives," unpublished essay, date unknown.

Cummings, William. *Making Blood White: Historical Transformations in Early Modern Makassar*. Honolulu: University of Hawaii Press, 2002.

Davis, Randall. *Digital Dilemma: Strategic Issues in Archiving and Accessing Digital Motion Picture Materials*. Academy of Motion Picture Arts and Sciences, 2007, http://www.oscars.org/science-technology/council/projects/digitaldilemma/.Decherney, Peter. *Hollywood and the Culture Elite: How the Movies Became American*. New York: Columbia University Press, 2005.

Deming, Barbara. "The Library of Congress Film Project: Exposition of a Method." *Library of Congress Quarterly Journal of Current Acquisitions* 2 (1944): 3–36.

Dempsey, Michael. "Colorization." *Film Quarterly* 40 (Winter 1986–87): 2–3.

Derrida, Jacques. *Archive Fever: A Freudian Impression*. Translated by Eric Prenowitz. Chicago: University of Chicago Press, 1995.

Dirks, Nicholas. "The Crimes of Colonialism: Anthropology and the Textualization of India." In *Colonial Subjects: Essays in the Practical History of Anthropology*, edited by Peter Pels and Oscar Salemink. Ann Arbor: University of Michigan Press, 1999.

Eiland, Howard. "Reception in Distraction." *boundary 2, no.* 30 (2003): 51–66.

Foucault, Michel. *Discipline and Punish: The Birth of the Prison*. New York: Pantheon, 1977.

———. *Madness and Civilization: A History of Insanity in the Age of Reason*. New York: Vintage, 1988.

———. *The Order of Things: An Archeology of the Human Sciences*. London: Tavistock, 1974.

Gaddis, John Lewis. *The Landscape of History: How Historians Map the Past*. Oxford, U.K.: Oxford University Press, 2002.

Geary, Patrick J. *Phantoms of Remembrance: Memory and Oblivion at the End of the First Millennium*. Princeton, N.J.: Princeton University Press, 1994.

Goodrum, Charles. *The Library of Congress*. New York: Praeger, 1974.

Gracy, Karen F. "Documenting Communities of Practice: Making the Case for Archival Ethnography." *Archival Science* 4 (2004): 335–65.

Grainge, Paul. *Monochrome Memories: Nostalgia and Style in Retro America*. Westport, Conn.: Praeger, 2002.

Greetham, David. "'Who's In, Who's Out': The Cultural Poetics of Archival Exclusion." *Studies in the Literary Imagination* 32 (1999): 1–28.

Grimm, Charles. "A Paper Print Pre-history." *Film History* 11 (1999): 204–16.

Hansen, Miriam Bratu. "America, Paris, the Alps: Kracauer and Benjamin on Cinema and

Modernity." In *Cinema and the Invention of Modern Life*, edited by Leo Charney and Vanessa Schwartz, Berkeley: University of California Press, 1995.

Hart, Justin. "Making Democracy Safe for the World: Race, Propaganda, and the Transformation of US Foreign Policy during World War II." *Pacific Historical Review* 73 (2004): 49–84.

Herrick, Doug. "Toward a National Film Collection: Motion Pictures at the Library of Congress." *Film Library Quarterly* 5 (1980): 5–23.

"History and Motion Pictures." *Views and Film Index* 1 (December 1, 1906): 1.

Horak, Jan-Christopher. "Film History and Film Preservation: Reconstructing the Text of *The Joyless Street* (1925)." *Screening the Past* 5 (1998), http://www.latrobe.edu.au/screeningthepast/.

Horne, Jennifer. "Experiments in Propaganda: Reintroducing James Blue's Colombia Trilogy." *Moving Image* (2009): 183–200.

Jensen, Richard. "The Culture Wars, 1965–1995: A Historian's Map." *Journal of Social History* 29 (1995): 17–37.

Koppes, Clayton, and Gregory Black. "What to Show the World: The Office of War Information and Hollywood, 1942–1945." *Journal of American History* 64 (1977): 87–105.

Kracauer, Siegfried. *Theory of Film: The Redemption of Physical Reality*. Princeton, N.J.: Princeton University Press, 1997.

Kula, Sam. "Introduction: Moving Image/American Image." In *The American Film Heritage: Impressions from the American Film Institute Archives*, edited by Kathleen Karr. Washington D.C.: American Film Institute, 1972.

Levine, Phillipa. "Discipline and Pleasure: Response." *Victorian Studies* 46 (2004): 319–25.

Lindquist, Jason. "'The Mightiest Instrument of the Physical Discoverer': The Visual 'Imagination' and the Victorian Observer." *Journal of Victorian Culture* 13 (2008): 171–99.

Lowenthal, David. *The Past is a Foreign Country*. Cambridge: Cambridge University Press, 1985.

Lynch, Michael. "Archives in Formation: Privileged Spaces, Popular Archives, and Paper Trails." *History of the Human Sciences* 12 (1999): 65–87.

MacLeish, Archibald. *Annual Report of the Librarian of Congress, 1942*. Washington, D.C.: U.S. Government Printing Office, 1943.

Mann, Sarah Ziebell. "The Evolution of American Moving Image Preservation: Defining the Preservation Landscape, 1967–1977." *Moving Image* 1 (2001): 1–20.

Manoff, Marlene. "Theories of the Archives from Across the Disciplines." *portal: Libraries and the Academy* 4 (2004): 9–25.

Mathur, Soloni. "History and Anthropology in South Asia: Rethinking the Archive." *Annual Review of Anthropology* 29 (2000): 89–106.

May, Lary. *Screening Out the Past: The Birth of Mass Culture and the Motion Picture Industry*. Chicago: University of Chicago Press, 1980.

McGreevey, Tom, and Joanne Yeck. *Our Movie Heritage*. New Brunswick, N.J.: Rutgers University Press, 1997.

Melville, Annette, and Scott Simmon. *Film Preservation 1993: A Study of the Current State of American Film Preservation*. Washington, D.C.: U.S. Government Printing Office, 1993.

Mohan, Jennifer. *Environmental Scan of Moving Image Collections in the United States.* Digital Library Federation, 2008, http://www.scribd.com/doc/5347688/Lot49.

Mulvey, Laura. *Death 24x a Second: Stillness and the Moving Image.* London: Reaktion Books, 2006.

Naremore, James. "Authorship." In *A Companion to Film Theory,* edited by Toby Miller and Robert Stam, 13–14. Malden, Mass.: Blackwell, 1999.

Nora, Pierre. *Realms of Memory: Rethinking the French Past.* Vol. 1. New York: Columbia University Press, 1992.

Peck, Gregory. Foreword to *The American Film Heritage: Impressions from the American Film Institute Archives,* by Tom Shales, 5. Washington D.C.: American Film Institute, 1972.

Ray, Robert B. *How a Film Theory Got Lost and Other Mysteries in Cultural Studies.* Bloomington: Indiana University Press, 2001.

Rosen, Philip. *Change Mummified: Cinema, Historicity, Theory.* Minneapolis: University of Minnesota Press, 2001.

———. Introduction to *boundary* 2, no. 30 (2003): 1–15.

Schwartz, Vanessa R. "Walter Benjamin for Historians." *American Historical Review* 106 (2001): 1721–43.

Slide, Anthony. *Nitrate Won't Wait: A History of Film Preservation in the United States.* Jefferson, N.C. : McFarland, 1992.

Spehr, Paul. "It Was Fifty Years Ago This Month: Motion Picture Division Celebrates its Golden Anniversary." *Library of Congress Information Bulletin* 51 (April 20, 1992): 175.

Stoler, Ann Laura. "Colonial Archives and the Arts of Governance." *Archival Science* 2 (2002): 87–109.

Tilton, Peter, Charles Martin, Jr., and Carleton Green. *Organization and Location of the American Film Institute.* South Pasadena, Calif.: Stanford Research Institute, 1967.

Usai, Paolo Cherchi. *The Death of Cinema: History, Cultural Memory, and the Digital Dark Age.* London: BFI, 2001.

Van Camp, Julie C. "Colorization Revisited." *Journal of Value Inquiry* 29 (December 1995): 448–68.

Voss, Paul J., and Marta L. Werner. "Toward a Poetics of the Archive." *Studies in the Literary Imagination* 32 (1999): i–viii.

Wagoner, Phillip B. "Precolonial Intellectuals and the Production of Colonial Knowledge." *Comparative Studies in Society and History* 45 (2003): 783–814.

Walls, Howard L. "Motion Picture Incunabula in the Library of Congress." *Journal of the Society of Motion Picture Engineers* 42 (1944): 155–58.

Wasson, Haidee. *Museum Movies: The Museum of Modern Art and the Birth of Art Cinema.* Berkeley: University of California Press, 2005.

———. "'Some Kind of Racket': The Museum of Modern Art's Film Library, Hollywood and the Problem of Film Art, 1935." *Canadian Journal of Film Studies* 9 (2000): 5–29.

Wostry, Nikolaus. "Sodom and Gomorrah: Notes on a Reconstruction, or Less is More." Translated by Jan-Christopher Horak. *Moving Image* 3 (2003): 19–39.

Young, Colin. "An American Film Institute: A Proposal." *Film Quarterly* 14 (1961): 37–50.

Zizek, Slavoj. *Looking Awry: An Introduction to Jacques Lacan through Popular Culture.* Cambridge, Mass.: MIT Press, 1992.

INDEX

JANNA JONES is professor in the School of Communication at Northern Arizona University. She is the author of *The Southern Movie Palace: Rise, Fall, and Resurrection.*

The University Press of Florida is the scholarly publishing agency for the State University System of Florida, comprising Florida A&M University, Florida Atlantic University, Florida Gulf Coast University, Florida International University, Florida State University, New College of Florida, University of Central Florida, University of Florida, University of North Florida, University of South Florida, and University of West Florida.

www.ingramcontent.com/pod-product-compliance
Lightning Source LLC
LaVergne TN
LVHW050955080826
845145LV00006B/1512

* 9 7 8 0 8 1 3 0 6 0 3 7 8 *